P9-CCA-786

THE
COKEVILLE
MIRACLE

HARTT WIXOM & **JUDENE WIXOM**

THE
COKEVILLE
MIRACLE

WHEN
ANGELS INTERVENE

Plain Sight Publishing
An Imprint of Cedar Fort Publishing, Inc. • Springville, Utah

© 2015 Hartt and Judene Wixom
Cover photo of children and photos from the film *The Cokeville Miracle* are courtesy of Remember Films, copyright 2015.

All rights reserved.

No part of this book may be reproduced in any form whatsoever, whether by graphic, visual, electronic, film, microfilm, tape recording, or any other means, without prior written permission of the publisher, except in the case of brief passages embodied in critical reviews and articles.

The opinions and views expressed herein belong solely to the author and do not necessarily represent the opinions or views of Cedar Fort, Inc. Permission for the use of sources, graphics, and photos is also solely the responsibility of the author.

ISBN 13: 978-1-4621-1761-1

Published by Plain Sight Publishing, an imprint of Cedar Fort, Inc.
2373 W. 700 S., Springville, UT 84663
Distributed by Cedar Fort, Inc., www.cedarfort.com

Library of Congress Card Catalog Number: 94-71254

Cover design by Lauren Error
Cover design © 2015 by Lyle Mortimer
Edited and typeset by Deborah Spencer

Printed in the United States of America

10 9 8 7 6 5 4 3 2 1

Printed on acid-free paper

Contents

Acknowledgments

The list of acknowledgments could be a long one. Special mention, however, must be made to the hostages, their families, and their friends, many of whom allowed us to interview them extensively. Key information about David and Doris Young, and their daughter Princess, (not attributed in the chapters themselves) was provided by special investigator Ron Hartley and the Lincoln County Sheriff's Office. Data on the bomb that had destroyed a school bus when detonated by David Young at his residence in Tucson, Arizona—but failed to explode as designed in the Cokeville Elementary School—was provided by Richard Haskell, explosives expert in Sweetwater County, Wyoming.

Eyewitness information was given by our son, Kamron, one of the hostages. We also appreciate the computer assistance provided by our daughter Peggy Proffit.

Key photos were made available courtesy of the Salt Lake City *Deseret News* and the *Star Valley Independent* newspaper. T. C. Christensen, who made the movie *The Cokeville Miracle*, assisted us with other photographs and his own research data. Lynnae Allred of Cedar Fort Publishing and Media and Lisa Williams provided much appreciated technical assistance. And Deborah Spencer and Lauren Error helped in the publishing process of this edition. We also join many others in commending filmmaker T. C. Christensen for the sensitivity and care shown in his movie as well as counseling with the survivors in the process of scripting *The Cokeville Miracle*.

Carla Toomer, Susan Fiscus, and Chemene Peterson, from the

Acknowledgments

Cokeville Miracle Foundation, who compiled the book *Witness to Miracles,* were immensely helpful in gathering dozens of individual testimonies about the historical events of May 16, 1986.

We must also thank the children who braved the ordeal against an evil force. As one said, "We were saved by angels. Now, we need to show our gratitude by the way we conduct the rest of our lives."

Our heartfelt support goes out to all who still struggle with scars—both emotional and physical—from the violence perpetrated on them as innocent children. Time alone is not always healing; compassion, love, and prayer can help.

Introduction

While the Cokeville Elementary School standoff includes elements of fear, terror, and cruelty, it also includes love, faith, and community-wide grit. At stake were the lives of 134 school children—almost every youngster in an entire Wyoming valley between the ages of five and twelve. This is their story.

Our greatest concern was in carefully researching the facts. They tell a dynamic story of the power of prayer. There is no need for dramatization or exploitation. Those testimonies speak for themselves. Initial news reports did tend to sensationalize. Time was required to sort some of them out.

In compiling this book, we faced a challenge not experienced by most writers. One of the hostages was our son. It made the challenge more insightful and also more difficult. The movie *The Cokeville Miracle* highlights many of those challenges and how the community of Cokeville met them. We thank the makers of this movie for their professionalism. Many Cokeville residents and former hostages found participation in the making of the film to be therapeutic. During a special screening of the movie, filmmaker T. C. Christensen voiced appreciation for the magnificent power of prayer. It was a message participants felt and appreciated.

Chapter One

"Me, God"

The children playing on the playground of Wyoming's Cokeville Elementary School had no idea as they went to class that day that they were being closely watched. From an observation post on Cemetery Hill, David Gary Young stepped from behind a small copse of cottonwood trees and adjusted his binoculars to get an unobstructed view of most of the field. The children, oblivious to his presence, had no idea that, for the past several years, Young had been as interested in their future as any of their teachers were. While the older kids were having their lunch recess and the little ones were on their way to afternoon class, Young observed the midday bustle from his hilltop hideout, and there he waited, observing and preparing.

It is doubtful that any of the children would have recognized him, or even noticed anything strange about David Young if they had met him in person, but their parents would have recognized this bearded man with a concentrated gaze and suspicious demeanor. Young had been the marshal of Cokeville several years earlier. His law enforcement career there had lasted a mere six months before he was fired.

Was David's nefarious return to Cokeville because he was angry at being terminated as marshal? Or was his unusual behavior while marshal a precursor of what was driving him now? "He always wore a gun in a holster tied down to his leg," one longtime citizen recalled. "He loved to wear big hats and straddle a chair backward like the old barroom cowboys in movies." He would often sit like that on the porch of the old Stockman's Hotel. John Dayton, mayor of Cokeville at the time, was concerned with

Young's interest in gathering firearms around himself and "giving out tickets for trivial things." He seemed to enjoy the power his title gave him without particularly worrying about the responsibility of it. "Young was fired," said Mayor Dayton, "because he cared more about dressing up like Wyatt Earp and swaggering around town with a show of guns than in actually enforcing the law." Town council members said Young was his own authority: "He didn't like to take orders," Dayton added. "He wouldn't."

David's first wife was the mother of his two daughters, Princess and Angela, and she remembers that disagreeing with him was dangerous. "He was always fascinated with firearms, physical force, and violence," she said. "He was for real. I was always frightened of him. One didn't get in his way, and I certainly didn't." She described him as an avid reader of misanthropic sociology books and white supremacist literature, but he never joined any organizations. All who knew him described him as a "loner."

Apparently, David had little trouble getting jobs, but staying with them was another matter. He had as many as sixteen jobs in eleven years. Occasionally, he would supplement earnings by selling one of his many guns.

He also kept copious journals, making certain that his life was well documented, apparently feeling anything he did was worthy of historical record. "Had a sip of coffee. Took a bite of donut, looked out the window, then had another sip of coffee," he would write. But many who knew him said that he had a "brilliant mind," a mathematical mind that could add up numbers in his head faster than anyone else could do so with paper and pencil. Perhaps it was just his absolute egotism that prompted the need to record everything he did. He made it clear that he felt his mind superior to all philosophies.

One of his most consistent passions was trying to mathematically disprove the existence of God, a theme throughout all of his diaries and journals. One of the bleakest entries he ever penned seems to reveal an inner confusion underscoring the outward contempt he showed for the concept of deity: "God is infinite, therefore God is nothing. Mathematically, God plus a pissant equals a pissant." In one journal entry, however, he added this: "Me, God."

Young had some physical problems, mostly associated with diabetes and the need for regular insulin injections. He drank alcohol sparingly, and there was no issue with drugs; he "didn't want anything to pollute his mind." On the surface, David seemed to be doing reasonably well, but underneath, his thinking was anything but reasonable.

For example, David developed an admiration for Adolph Hitler, who had promised to lead the German nation out of its humiliating past to a new existence of superiority, security, and abundance. When he could not achieve these goals through diplomacy and the mutual consent of Germany's neighbors, Hitler was perfectly willing to use guns and bombs to force them into obedience. David apparently saw only strength in such ruthlessness. Such unilateral self-centeredness would have seemed to him merely right and proper, the natural behavior of a "superior" man.

Another example of his wrong-minded thinking was his twisted relationship with his own daughters, both of them born during his marriage to his first wife. Angela and Princess both reported that their father earned extra cash by selling nude photos of them. Their grandfather confirmed this, saying that David had peddled the photos for whatever money they might bring in. David's involvement in this kind of behavior continued for many years. His refusal to change these habits caused increasingly strained relations between him and most of his kin. Angela announced one day in her early teens that she couldn't live with her father's irrational edicts any longer, departed with little fanfare, and did not return.

While David lived in Cokeville, he became acquainted with Doris Young, a woman six years older than he, who would become his second wife.

Doris had divorced her second husband and moved to Cokeville a year earlier to live near her daughter, Bernie. After a tragic accident took the life of Doris's son, she became bitter and decided there was no God. Part of the attraction between David and Doris was this shared atheistic inclination. They also shared a belief in reincarnation and, according to Bernie, "had no particular fear of death." David's philosophy was that we "'perceive' ourselves to be here, and so we are here. Man exists in his own mind. Then, we had to perceive a master, and so we made up a god. God is just in our minds," he would emphasize. "Infinity was just in our heads," Bernie explained.

When David Young left Cokeville after being fired as town marshal, Doris climbed on the back of his motorcycle and went along for the ride.

They settled in Arizona. Eventually, David got to the point where work was "interfering with his thinking" and income was up to Doris. She sang at bars and did housecleaning for others. She was considered by her coworkers and neighbors to be a nice person, but one acquaintance commented, "That David, I didn't like him at all."

"The Biggie"

As he withdrew more and more from society, David's declarations of belief became increasingly rambling, confused, and almost always critical of the human race. A growing bitterness against society and government intensified over the years. All this was documented in his journals, eventually totaling forty-one volumes. Within these handwritten records, he brooded over the tyranny, as he saw it, of adhering to laws and rules, whether those of man or those of God. He grew determined to take action, and a diabolical plan began to take shape.

He began referring to his emerging plan of action as "the Biggie"—something that would make everyone realize how serious, how superior, and how correct he was about life, reality, and the nature of human existence. Diary entries confirm that he didn't see his plan as anything wrong, let alone irrational. He was a man whose sometimes charismatic and probative intellect often attracted people, people who thought him bright and capable of accomplishing much. By 1986, however, David's thinking was the product of years of inner loneliness, brooding grudges, preoccupation with self-godhood, and distrust of outside thought.

David Young's repulsion for people he considered less intelligent than himself was about to explode into action. His "Biggie" would be to descend upon the unsuspecting community of Cokeville and take the children away from their "corrupt" teachers and government officials into a "Brave New World." Here, he would be their "Lord and Master." These children would be the ideal subjects for him to tutor as reincarnated spirits because, as he had observed, they were bright children, and this close-knit community would be willing to pay a hefty ransom to get them back. This was the reason he waited on the hillside, binoculars in hand, watching.

As events would prove, he had no intention to release his hostages, money or no money. Evidence from his journals indicates that he had convinced Doris that they could take the town's ransom money, as well as his own extensive collection of guns and journals, with the children into his own kingdom beyond the "abysmal nihility" of earthly existence.

He felt he had to kill the children to gain an afterlife control of their minds. They had to die so that he could take them to a "better" world where, under his rule, they might live in a wonderful reincarnated state. He wanted young, trusting, and obedient children to people his new world so he could teach them to be smart—like himself.

This diabolical plan would have to be accomplished in one dramatic action, like an all-consuming explosion filling the air with searing flame. Of course, this needed to be practiced to meet the perfection his ego demanded. To fund all this, he needed to bring "investors" into the scheme, and he eventually found three who were adequately impressed with his intellect to believe he could come up with something worth paying into. With the promise of "making millions," Gerald Deppe, Doyle Mendenhall, and Robert Harrison trusted the greater intelligence of their friend and were apparently OK with his assertion that he would share the details of his plan with them at a later date. Meanwhile, he started testing his plan. He assembled bomb-making components and eventually found an abandoned school bus in the desert near Tucson, Arizona, where he detonated a test bomb. One quick flip of the trigger and the entire vehicle exploded in flame and blasted a huge ball of fire into the sky. "It worked perfectly!" he wrote in his journal. He was ready to head for Cokeville with his bomb.

On Wednesday, May 14, David wrote in his journal, "And the plot thickens. Slept decently for as excited as I was. Up at 0700 and into day. . . . My mind is going from thought to thought, trying to keep everything in order. Nice weather. Dorsie and I into Cokeville."

He noted that two of his investor friends had now joined him and that they were "still full of fun and lots of laughs." His friends were excited to learn, at last, just how they were going to make their millions. But Young still kept the plan to himself. Uncomfortable with being kept in the dark, the third investor, Robert Harrison, opted to back out and returned home. Since he knew nothing that could interfere with the plan, Young allowed him to leave. The other two, although perhaps now more curious than ever, stayed on. At some point, Princess had joined the group, obviously at David's invitation or urging. Meanwhile, Doris noted in her journal, "I wonder what they will call us in the Brave New World."

On the morning of the sixteenth of May, the five remaining members of the group climbed into a white van, windows obscured with white paint per David's orders, and headed into the last lap for Cokeville. Somewhere along US 30, David stopped to make a voice recording of exactly what was about to take place. This was the first the investors heard of the planned "revolution," and they immediately stated they could not be a part of it. But now they knew too much. David refused to let them go. He pulled a gun on his two friends, ordering Doris and Princess to handcuff them to the inside of the van. They might have refused to cooperate, but he would make sure they couldn't interfere. It had now become clear that painting the windows white would not only obscure the arsenal of weapons contained therein, but also the two men who were no longer useful in David's sinister plan. He had just taken his first two hostages.

The bomb had been assembled into a two-wheel shopping cart, meticulously wired together. The design was to detonate five blasting caps, three on one shelf and two on a lower shelf, all sparked by an electric charge from a battery. The caps, each set into a can filled with gun powder, aluminum dust, and flour, were designed to blow their component particles into the air like confetti. A gallon of gasoline would explode and ignite the air-borne particles. The results could "blow up an entire room of medium size, cave in the walls, and kill everyone in it." The trigger was a simple device using a clothespin that would snap when pulled. According to experts, this type of mechanism is called a "deadman's switch" because if the person holding it goes down, the bomb will detonate. That was exactly what David wanted. The last component to be added to the bomb was the gallon of gasoline, and David stopped to search the Cokeville landfill to find a plastic jug.

David had crossed the line from eccentric philosopher to a guerrilla terrorist. He was a dangerous man with a deadly weapon. Now, all he had to do was wait for the lunch hour to end and for the children to be gathered inside the schoolhouse.

Chapter Two

A Town of Trust

Exactly what kind of a town was Cokeville, Wyoming, and why, of all of the communities he could target, did David Young choose this one?

With a population of approximately five hundred residents, Cokeville is different, in many ways, from even its closest Mountain West neighbors. Once known as "Sheep Capital of the West," several dance halls, including one in the Stockman Hotel, provided entertainment for the large number of cowboys who gathered in season with their flocks. Cokeville today is home mostly to cattle ranchers and their families. The train that used to bring or load sheep by the thousands still runs through the west side of town, but it no longer stops, and the dance halls are gone.

Battling icy roads in the long, relentless winters does not dampen the enthusiasm of Cokeville's citizens for their town. Winter nights have been known to hit 40 degrees below zero, and the high mountain winds add to the chill. Residents generally joke that snow never melts in Wyoming's hills; it just blows around until it wears out.

While it is an isolated community, the history of the untamed West didn't bypass Cokeville. Even now, hills in the border area around the town's outskirts yield remnants of old stills from the Prohibition years. There were once five busy dance halls in the town itself. A visitor may see mule deer, Canada geese, or sandhill cranes in the cultivated fields, and even elk or moose on the outskirts of town. Tourists come to fish for trout in the Bear River and Smiths Fork, or to ride the ski lift in Pine Creek Canyon. Family-owned ranches dotted with mostly black Angus cattle stay green in the summer via rolling sprinkler irrigation systems.

Youngsters in Cokeville don't have much time to be idle. Some of them drive tractors before they are big enough to see over the dashboard of the family car. Even the little ones help keep irrigation schedules running or get the hay in. Many of the children know what it's like to be responsible for raising chickens, pigs, or steers as they participate in an active 4H program that helps them earn money for their future education. The refinements of sewing, art, and photography are also encouraged, because the community has a proud history of successful artists. In the summer, the library hosts a well-attended and active children's reading program, evidence of the community's commitment to successfully educating the next generation.

There is still no movie theater, video arcade, or game center for young people to gather in. Their time and energies are consumed by mostly ranching and school activities. There is little need to focus on what some parents strive to do in "building character." It is built in. Some are up early for ranch chores, then school and all its extracurricular activities, and on weekends, there are church obligations and more ranch chores.

While there are plenty of chores to go around, community members are quick to join together for community-wide entertainment and events. Annual expeditions to gather firewood for the widows always conclude with a hearty Dutch oven supper. Smiths Fork, which runs through town, provides fishing competition for youngsters.

Homecoming Week at the high school involves the whole community. Students past and present work on the festivities, planning or marching in the parade or climbing Big Hill to help light the block "C." Just about everyone comes to the barbecue in the park preceding the exuberant pep rally and bonfire. Every game day always brings out a big local crowd, including games as far away as several hundred miles, more evidence of the close-knit community.

For many years, all school students met in one building, but a new elementary school was opened one year before Young returned to town. The kids were proud to have their own school now, and they were aware of the tradition of high academic achievement in the community. They knew that the graduating class from the previous year had sent 96 percent of their graduates to college, most on some kind of scholarship.

Generally considered a religious community with a friendly mix of Mormon, Catholic, and Protestant citizens, there were also a few who described themselves as "agnostic," including Rocky Moore, a genuine mountain man who spent much of this time shooting an old-fashioned musket, rarely missing. Moore said he would believe in a divine power when he saw "the burning bush." He would have more to say about that after May 16.

Music teacher John Miller was of Methodist stock, but with no Methodist church in town, he worshipped with the Episcopalians. When the high school produced *The Sound of Music* one year, the Mormon mothers who were pitching in to help with costumes recruited the Catholic home economics teacher, Clara Dayton, to learn how to make a nun's habit. In a predominantly religious community, it was noted with a sense of pride that during the annual Pioneer Day celebration, the spectators at the town rodeo might watch while a self-described agnostic helped a Catholic youngster, encouraged by a Protestant cowboy, onto a feisty calf provided by a Mormon bishop.

While it may be impossible to determine exactly why Young chose Cokeville as the target of his plan, evidence suggests that there were essentially four reasons this community was the perfect place to stage "The Biggie":

- It was a town made up of trusting, generally religious individuals who felt safe enough in their own community that they seldom locked the doors to their homes.
- It was an isolated community with only two policemen. Young knew it would take time to amass a contingency of law enforcement capable of stopping him.
- It was a close-knit community with people who knew one another by name and would be fiercely protective of their children—even to the point of paying a hefty ransom.
- It was a community that made every effort to raise hard-working, highly intelligent children.

David Young may not have noted all this, but he did write in his lengthy journal that it was a closely bonded "town of trust." That much he had noticed while twirling pistols on the Stockman's Hotel veranda. And for these reasons and others, Cokeville was picked as the perfect location to pull off "The Biggie."

Chapter Three

A Town without Children

"There is no doubt in my mind that David Young planned to kill the children to gain control of their minds."

—Ron Hartley, sheriff's investigator

On the afternoon of May 16, 1986, afternoon kindergarten was about to start. Jeremiah Moore was excited about school that day—it was also his seventh birthday. Little Jody Pope arrived a bit early for kindergarten and headed for her class with Mrs. Petersen. A mother of five, Carol Petersen believed in firm discipline, but she found her charges' natural curiosity a better method for keeping them interested, especially when the topic, as it would be today, was dinosaurs. Jody loved Mrs. Petersen's classes and looked forward to studying the awesome creatures with the magical names. Shiloh Pope, Jody's seven-year-old brother, liked school but was happiest at work on the ranch. Already he rode his horse well enough to help round up stray cows on the range. Still, Shiloh was a good role model for Jody. Last year, she had watched him enviously as he brought beginning reading books home from Mrs. Janel Dayton's first-grade class. Now Jody was learning to read and just couldn't wait to learn more.

The Pope kids were close friends with the Wixoms, and Jody's face lit up when she saw sixth-grader Kamron Wixom on the playground. Kam had recently been the lead in the elementary school production of *Tom Sawyer*, a good outlet for a boy with a penchant for mimicking well-known characters. Kam's friend, Travis Walker, had played Huck Finn. The whole town loved the show. Travis's parents, Kevin and Glenna, had recently completed emergency medical training and felt prepared to face their first on-call challenge.

Another student, fourth-grader Rusty Birch, had done a great job playing Winthrop in the high school production of *The Music Man*. Gina Taylor, winding up her first year in grade school, was the only girl in a family of four older brothers. She sang while the boys handled piano and several other instruments.

Just as Pat Bennion got her two girls off to catch the bus that morning, she received a call from the school. "Can you substitute for Mr. Teichert's third-grade class today? He has a track meet out of town." Having taken this class before, Pat readily agreed. "Sure, I'll be right there," she told them, and she was on her way as soon as she arranged for her son, Sam, to stay with a neighbor until it was time to catch the afternoon bus for his kindergarten class. Pat's mother-in-law, Verlene, was already there as a teacher's aide.

Paul Clark's mother, Eva, had just called the school that afternoon to say her son would be late. "I'll drive him in shortly," she said. "The bus won't need to make a trip up the canyon for him." The Clark family treated getting to and from school quite seriously. Eva and Lowell and their eight children were building a new log home, tucked in the pine trees and just behind a bend in the Smiths Fork River. It was as peaceful a place as existed anywhere, but it meant the school bus had to come ten miles each way to pick up their children.

And so went a typical day for this typical town, a close-knit community about to be pulled together tighter than they ever imagined.

***

Meanwhile, David Young parked his van in the school parking lot, and he, Doris, and Princess started unloading the arsenal of weapons and supplies. Princess did not share the irrational emotions of her father and began to feel as if she were caving under the strain of the last two days. At one point, David told her to move some of the guns. As she did, she dropped something. That did not escape the watchful eye of her father. He looked at his daughter coldly. "Screw up one more time," he announced tersely, "and I'll shoot you." She was certain he would.

With his two friends secured helplessly to the interior of the van, David now had only his obedient wife and nervous daughter to help carry in all the firearms: five rifles—including two AR-15 semi-automatics—five pistols, ample ammunition for all of them, plus additional ammo to be placed near the bomb so the searing heat of the blast would cause them to explode. In addition to the five blasting caps already part of the bomb assembly, another thirty were brought into the school.

The three must have made quite a sight, had anyone been outside to see them, as they made their way up the walk, the girls struggling with all the guns and David wheeling the cart full of assembled bomb components. A number of David's journals were also carted in. Apparently his understanding of reincarnation included the concept that his journals, filled with notations of his superior thoughts and actions, would also be restored into his Brave New World.

He had taken the time earlier to make copies of his mathematical treatise for eternal life via reincarnation, which he entitled "Zero Equals Infinity" (see Appendix V). He had already sent one to President Reagan so that he too would be enlightened. Young's convictions were firm. He had faith enough in his beliefs to act on them. Now he would put the plan in motion because he thought he had figured it out and was ready to die for a new and better world. Armed with a .22 pistol and a 9 mm tucked in his waistband, Young personally wheeled in the bomb. It was time to announce his presence.

***

Inside the school, the end of the south hallway turned right. David and his little group followed the turn and saw, near the front entrance, a counter and receptionist's desk next to the principal's office. Someone was seated at the desk.

Christina "Tina" Cook, the school receptionist, looked up as she heard someone approaching. Originally from Canada, she had moved from Washington, D.C., to Cokeville after David and Doris had moved away, so she had no reason to recognize any of the people coming down the hall, burdened with what looked like a stack of guns and something in a shopping cart. Casual attire and paraphernalia of one kind or another were familiar sights to anybody living in a rural, outdoor-active town, and their presence did not initially alarm her.

Tina greeted them as she would any other visitor to the school. "Hello," she said with her usual smile. There was no response from either the woman or girl. The man came closer and stood, also silently, just watching her. She was surprised at the grim look on his face. At almost the same moment, another woman approached the receptionist's desk. Tina assumed she was with the others because she had never seen this woman either.

This woman, Cindy Cowden, had an appointment with Principal Max Excell. She was there to interview for a teaching position that was open in the kindergarten. Since Mr. Excell was not in sight and the receptionist was busy with three other people, Cindy decided to step into the restroom.

Tina's attention came back to the three standing in front of her. The man was speaking. "Mrs. Cook," he said, scrutinizing her nameplate. "Is that your name?"

"Yes, it is. Can I help you?" Tina tried again to initiate a normal conversation.

"You certainly can," he responded, but said nothing more.

Tina had never seen so depressing and cheerless a look as the one on his face. With a shock, she understood it was really possible for a person to have "cold eyes."

The man leaned toward her. "Mrs. Cook, this is a revolution! This school is being taken hostage!"

Tina was unsure how to respond, and David must have seen she hadn't quite taken in his announcement. "Don't push any alarms, answer any phones, or call for help! We are very serious, Mrs. Cook. I have guns and this is a bomb." David opened his jacket and pointed clearly to the shoe-lace-trigger attached to his wrist and its connection to the shopping cart.

Tina looked from the pile of components back to David, still in disbelief.

He explained about the clothespin detonator. "See where I have inserted the plug between the two ends of the pin? I have only to let them touch, Mrs. Cook, and this entire building, with everyone in it, blows sky high. Mrs. Cook, you and I are only one-half inch from death."

Tina felt a spurt of anger. She wished he would stop saying her name like that, over and over again, especially in that sepulchral tone. She hadn't moved from the mean streets of Washington, D.C., to this rural haven where people raised families in love and respect just to be threatened at her desk by a rude, self-important stranger.

David must have seen the doubt in her eyes. Even more pointedly, he said, "Try to hit me on the head, jump me from behind, or anything at all, and I will pull this bomb trigger as I go down. Do I make myself clear, Mrs. Cook?"

He is making himself ridiculous, she thought, but she realized he saw himself much differently than that. She couldn't even think of how to respond.

"How many telephones do you have here in the school, Mrs. Cook?" he asked.

"Five," she managed to say.

"Well, unplug them. All five." She looked at him numbly for a minute and then got up and walked to the principal's office to comply. "Stop!" he suddenly shouted.

Doris came up to Tina and looked at her closely. "May I impress upon your mind, Mrs. Cook"—now she was doing it!—"that the lives of everyone in this building depend on what you do in the next several minutes?" Tina could only nod.

Just then, Cindy Cowden reappeared. She saw David gesture to her and said, "No, I'm fine. I'll just wait for Mr. Excell right here."

"Lady, you better get over here with the others," he replied.

Cindy didn't like being ordered around by this man. Again, she said, "No, I'll just wait right here." Without speaking, David lifted the barrel of his pistol and aimed it at her. She couldn't believe it. "What's this," she said, laughing, "a new interviewing technique?" Tina shook her head at Cindy, and the receptionist's terse expression sobered her immediately. As instructed, she joined the group.

At this moment, Janel Dayton came to the office to pick up her mail. She had been a Cokeville first-grade teacher for several years and had six children, her youngest in the morning kindergarten. Her husband ran their family ranch north of town. She took in the entourage with a look and decided she would just go back to her room and pick up her mail later.

Before she could, David turned and once more loudly announced, "This is a revolution!"

She turned back. "Who do you represent?" she asked him.

"Ourselves!" he said. Janel tried to walk away, but he stopped her. Like Tina and Cindy, she was soon made a part of the hostage group.

The next person to come upon the gathering was fifth-grade teacher

Rocky Moore, intent on getting some papers he wanted from his desk. Suddenly he heard an angry voice. "You! Get over here with the others behind this counter!"

A stocky and determined man—not the type to be bullied—he muttered, "That'll be the day!" and merely kept on going.

"I know you, Rocky!" the voice boomed. Moore stopped to see who was talking. As he walked back, he suddenly found himself looking down the barrel of a pistol, less than a foot away. Then the man who had spoken cocked the gun. It was so close Rocky could see the slug in firing position.

"You don't remember me," the man said. "But I'd just as soon kill you right now as later." He seemed really angry. "Get over here and keep quiet!"

Rocky shrugged his shoulders. "Okay. Hey, I'm coming, if that's the way you feel about it." He knew the tall man now. David had been his tenant years ago. There had been the usual disagreements about repairs and rent paid on time. David wanted more than repairs; he wanted remodeling. Rocky had told him he was free to leave. He thought little more about David once he moved away. But David clearly didn't forget him. He didn't like not getting his way. That wasn't the way things should be.

Rocky realized that confronting David now would only make matters worse. Since the man already bore him a grudge, Rocky decided to stay as quiet and inconspicuous as possible and wait the turn of events. David already seemed to have forgotten him anyway and was concentrating on looking for a bigger space to commandeer. He shepherded everyone toward the adjacent conference room. "Is that a large room?" he asked.

"No, it isn't," Tina said. Cindy Cowden and Janel Dayton were pushed right into the room. David kept the group together while he looked inside.

Cindy noticed an open window. She suggested to Janel that they climb out and run.

Janel thought about it seriously. But she had just turned over her first-grade class to fellow teacher Jean Mitchell for combined activities with Mrs. Mitchell's students. It was the first day of their trade arrangement, and both teachers were excited about the approach. Janel considered what might happen if the man found out she was missing and decided to take it out on Jean or any of the children. No, she decided, she would have to stay and see the whole thing through.

While David was looking over the accommodations, Princess was sent to the van to bring in more weapons. By the time she returned, a newcomer had joined the group—sixty-six-year-old teacher's aide Verlene Bennion. It was clear that the conference room would not be big enough for the number of people David intended to capture—many more than those taken hostage so far. Once everyone realized that the shopping cart held a genuine bomb and that he was ready to detonate it if crossed, it wasn't hard to herd them back down the south hallway, searching for the most appropriate room.

There are unanswered questions about what happened next. Tina Cook thought Princess was an enthusiastic conspirator, as guilty as David and Doris, of planning and executing the takeover of the school. Others felt her actions at this point showed that she was coerced into helping and had no wish to harm anyone.

Whatever her state of mind at the moment, she appeared to have come to some kind of breaking point. Several in the group heard her say to David, "My God! My God! I can't believe you would do this to innocent children!" Then she simply turned and walked away.

David's reaction to this outburst is almost impossible to define. Hindsight suggests he could easily have lost control, ordering Princess to remain, and if further crossed, attacked her or one of the innocent bystanders, perhaps even setting off the bomb. Perhaps she would have given in and obeyed his orders if he had simply cowed her with verbal threats. Perhaps he saw something in his daughter's face that no one else could and knew she was more dangerous to his plans if she stayed than if she left. Whatever the case, witnesses all agree that he tossed the van keys to her and shouted, "Take these then and get the hell out of here!" She left the building immediately, taking with her David and Doris's only avenue of escape.

Quickly reasserting his authority after Princess's defection, David settled on the middle door of the hallway and told Doris to go round up the other children and bring them all to him. He stood at the entrance to Room 4, where Mrs. Mitchell was presenting a flannel-board story to her students, plus Janel Dayton's. After she finished "Goldilocks and the Three Bears," Jean Mitchell intended to move smoothly into a discussion of magnets and then into the kids' favorite discussion topic, dinosaurs. Later, they would practice arithmetic and spelling. The afternoon was well-planned, and the students seemed to be enjoying the story.

She was therefore a little irritated when a shaggy-looking man barged into her room, pulling a cart and surrounded by a group of people, some of whom she knew and some she had never seen before. She was even more surprised when the man began stacking rifles against her classroom wall. She quickly realized he had pistols tucked in his belt as well. Before she could adjust to the invasion, he was inside the room, as were the five other people with him, and he was sounding very much in charge.

Within a few minutes, a crowd of other students began streaming through her door, taking the papers being handed out to them by a woman Jean didn't know but who was obviously with the bearded man.

Doris had managed her task of gathering hostages well. Thinking her invitation to be on the orders of Principal Max Excell, several of the teachers she had confronted had willingly led their students to Room 4 when she told them they were to assemble there. Music teacher John Miller had been swept along with them. In minutes, Jean's room, designed for 30, held 135 children and 18 adults.

Ten-year-old Jerry Dayton was curious about what was going on. The lady had told his class, "Follow me! . . . I have a surprise for you!" When he got in the room and saw all the guns and the strange people, he remembered they had been studying Libya recently. Maybe the school had put together a kind of assembly to teach everybody how to defend themselves against terrorists. It was a neat idea.

The room David selected was good for his purposes. There was no door to the outside and the window sections that were movable were small, only opening partway. More and more self-assured as growing numbers of school children came under his gaze, David watched Doris hand out more of his pamphlets and waited for the commotion to die down.

Jean Mitchell wasn't ready to relinquish her classroom. "You've got to be kidding," she said. David scowled. "This is my room!" she pressed.

David wouldn't condescend to argue. "Sit down and shut up!" he told her, and there was no mistaking the implied threat.

Others were still being dragged into the situation. The special education teacher, Gloria Mower, was working one-on-one with a student in the adjoining room when the commotion began to distract her. Peeking into Room 4, she and her student were "invited" in.

Fourth-grade teacher Kliss Sparks, as much a grandmother to her students as their instructor, was treating the class to an outdoor session on the lawn, the perfect place to read out loud from *Tom Sawyer*. Hearing the noise inside, however, she thought perhaps she had missed word of a program of some kind intended for her students as well. She took the class in and found herself trapped with everyone else. Now she struggled to forgive herself for exposing her students to danger.

Sandy Gonzales, a UPS driver, came down the hall, looking for someone to accept her delivery. Soon she was one of the hostages.

Eva Clark, who had earlier called the school not to be worried about Paul being a bit late, had just arrived with him and was taking him to class. Her four-year-old, Kathy, was left in the car, since Eva would be right back. Arriving at Paul's classroom, she was surprised to find it empty. The library was vacant as well. Then she saw teacher Jack Mitchell coming down the hall. "They might be down in my wife's room," Jack told her with a laugh. "It looks like they've got something going on down there. Jean is always cooking up something new."

Eva and Paul went to Room 4, where the boy quickly found his classmates. The woman at the door beckoned Eva in as well. Intent on her afternoon tasks, Eva barely noticed her. Spring branding was scheduled to begin the next day, and she had shopping to do in Montpelier before she could even begin to help her husband, Lowell, bring the cattle in. Lots of relatives were coming, some from out of state. To host them properly and complete all the preparations, she would have to stick to her list.

"I've got to go," Eva smiled at the woman who had gestured to her.

"No, come in," the woman said. "You'll want to see this."

"I just haven't got the time," Eva tried to explain.

Again, the woman insisted. This time her expression was irritable rather than smiling.

Then Janel Dayton stepped in. "You may want to stay," she said quietly. "We have a problem here." Eva saw the pistols David was wearing and the shoelace-trigger attached to his wrist. Suddenly, Eva thought about the other five of her six children who were in the room. There was no question. She would have to stay.

School custodian Delbert Rentfro had not yet been seen by either David or Doris. He met up with Principal Max Excell and told him that the fifth graders were in their classroom but their teacher, Mr. Miller, wasn't there. "The kids are starting to get a bit noisy," he said.

Since it was unlike Mr. Miller, a much-respected music teacher on loan from the high school, to be tardy or absent without notice, Excell went to look for him. On the way, he observed the milling and confusion around Room 4. What he saw in the doorway made him even more concerned: an unauthorized assembly—an assembly, in fact, of most of the school, crammed together in one classroom! He spotted John Miller about the same time he realized something was wrong. "What is going on here?" he demanded.

David knew an authority figure when he saw one. "Are you the principal?" he asked.

Excell said yes and repeated his question. Getting no satisfactory answer, Excell sat down and studied the children. Many of them were attempting to play or read. He noticed they also frequently looked up at David and Doris, as if hoping they would be gone the next time they looked. The children were apparently quite aware of the cart and its importance and realized that David was consciously holding his hand low and quiet.

"I didn't get the feeling he was acting," said one child later. "He was too careful to keep his hand down all the time."

One of his friends explained, "A teacher told me that we needed to be quiet and not upset the man. One jerk from his wrist and the bomb would blow. I kept watching to see that he kept his wrist down."

Once Excell realized the gravity of the situation, he also realized that there were things they needed to have in the room if the adults were going to keep the children well and occupied. He asked David for permission to gather up boxes of tissue, aspirin, and other things needed to keep the children settled down. David told him he could have a few minutes, and the principal went out to forage.

When he came back, he learned that David had more plans for him. He named Excell his spokesman and told the principal to call authorities and state that he wanted two million dollars for each of the kids. "I want no part of the negotiations," said David. "They have a way of trying to break you down. I don't want to waste time with that. You do the talking."

Excell tried to keep his voice calm. Over a hundred kids meant over two hundred million dollars, just as a ballpark figure. What hope was there of getting that large a ransom? But he couldn't solve that part of it now. "Who do you want me to call first?" he asked David. "The sheriff?"

"That's fine," David replied benignly. "Tell them I'm prepared to be here ten days or more if necessary. It may take Congress that long to raise the money."

Excell thought the man was calm enough to risk a question: "Why this school?" he asked, keeping his voice low. "Why here?"

David was very willing to reply. "Because this is a family town," he said, "where people love their children, and they'll do anything to get them back." Unknown to Excell and the others, David was not just guessing. Later investigations proved that he had taken notes while living in Cokeville about the school children and their families, including things such as who was close friends with whom. David's answer to Excell was much more than a casual remark. In fact, it was a real conclusion David had drawn about the kind of people who inhabited this small—but in his eyes—unique western town.

As Excell got up to make his first outside call, David gave him a sharp warning. "Be back here every ten minutes to make your report, or I'll start shooting these kids one by one." Later, probably recognizing the impractical constraint he was placing on Excell, David allowed fifteen minutes instead of ten.

Excell left for his office to make the all-important call. He tried to compute the total dollar amount of David's ransom demand. It would be staggering, and probably impossible to get.

Inside his office, he called the sheriff's office and told them what was happening. He was surprised to learn they had just been contacted by someone else, a young woman calling herself Princess, who had made a "strange report" about a "hostage crisis" at the elementary school. Excell quickly confirmed her story. "It's happening to us. Right now!" he assured the sheriff's secretary.

Princess had indeed used her unexpected freedom not to disappear into safe anonymity but to go for help. With Deppe and Mendenhall still shackled in the van, she swiftly drove to the town hall two blocks west and burst hysterically through the first door she saw, confronting a startled clerk. "Is there a police officer here?" she demanded.

Nadine Dana said there was not. "Maybe I can help you," she offered. No, Princess wanted a policeman. Nadine said she thought she could handle it.

Frustrated, Princess poured out her incredible tale. She was excited and difficult to understand—sometimes rambling and profane. The noise brought city employee Kevin Walker over, where he took the stranger aside. "We don't talk like that around here," he admonished her.

"Don't you folks care about your children?" Princess demanded. She looked back and forth at the two city workers and tried to order her thoughts so she could communicate with them. "My father has a bomb, and he is going to blow up the grade school!" Mrs. Dana felt sick. She had twin daughters in third grade, and she knew the other children as well. Kevin Walker had three children, Travis, Kathy, and Rachel. From his expression, it was clear Kevin also realized that, whoever the woman was, she was totally serious.

Across the hall, an emergency-strategy meeting was just breaking up. Wyoming regional watermaster, John Teichert, and Civil Defense and US Army Corp of Engineers officials were discussing a flood that was threatening north-side residents along Smiths Fork. Having decided on the appropriate emergency measures, the corpsmen had already left for their homes. Teichert, who lived in Cokeville, and the Civil Defense workers, who (like the corpsmen) all lived in other parts of the state, were just about to leave.

They came out of their meeting to the news that the elementary school was under siege. The urgency of the flood suddenly vanished. Teichert was not only the regional watermaster but also a lifelong resident of the town and a local Mormon bishop. A number of the students were in his congregation; he knew most of the kids in town by name.

As the scope and danger of their problem became clear to him, his first impulse was to pray. Seeking out a private room downstairs, Teichert pleaded for the Lord to intervene in some way for the sake of the children. "I emphasized how every child in there was vital to this community," Teichert said. "I told God we would do all we could, but we would need His help."

The Civil Defense workers, Kathy Davison, Bob Looney, and Grant Sorensen, immediately began making emergency contacts. Davison had been a sheriff's dispatcher, so she had considerable experience obtaining the needed help. With the aid of Mrs. Dana, they alerted ambulances in Cokeville and Lincoln County, at the county seat of Kemmerer and at Afton, both communities about fifty miles away. Davison then tried to locate the four law enforcement officers who lived in Cokeville. Through luck or prior planning on David's part, the four were all out of town. Sheriff's Deputy Ron Hartley was on his day off, as was local Police Chief Cal Fredrickson. Wyoming Highway Patrolman Brad Anderson was located via radio near Kemmerer, where he was patrolling. Sheriff's Deputy Earl Carroll lived in Cokeville but was working in Kemmerer as well that day. He was the first lawman to reach the town hall.

By the time Deputy Carroll arrived, Max Excell's first contact with the sheriff's department had been made. The authorities learned quickly that they had better not let themselves be seen near the school building. David had promised, through Excell, that he would start shooting if anyone appeared. Princess confirmed that her father was fully capable of doing just that. Warnings to keep their distance from the school were relayed to each new official as he or she arrived. Officer Carroll understood what Principal Excell was trying to tell him. "You're there and we aren't," he told Excell. "We'll take our cues from you. But . . . damn!"

Even with this warning, it was imperative to get close enough to the school to make some kind of informed analysis about the situation there. The new building grounds were almost bare; there was just flat lawn all the way to the fence. Part of the boundary abutted Art Robinson's backyard. Eventually, officers tried to see into Room 4 using binoculars from a position behind Art's fence. Officers risked being easily seen if they moved while someone was looking out the window. But the officers themselves could only see vague figures moving about through the narrow, horizontal windows. It wasn't helpful.

During the interval after Deputy Carroll was located and before he arrived, Princess found the key to the handcuffs, finally allowing Deppe and Mendenhall to be released. Princess's description of the morning of the takeover had basically exonerated them, but all three were, in effect, detained so that they could provide as much information as possible. John Teichert volunteered to keep an eye on them until Carroll and more deputies arrived. Deppe and Mendenhall were then questioned to glean every possible detail about David Young and his scheme.

Princess's information was particularly alarming. She described the number and kind of weapons she had helped carry into the school and the kind of bomb David was using. It became clear that the takeover was a true case of terrorism. When Deputy Carroll arrived, he remained at the town hall to coordinate emergency operations. Davison and

---

others alerted the Sweetwater County Sheriff's Office, including bomb expert Rich Haskell; Teton County's SWAT Team; Bear Lake County, Idaho's Sheriff Brent Bunn and his deputies; and men from the sheriff's department in Rich County, Utah. Neighboring counties also promised help, if needed.

Since hostage-taking had been made a federal offense in 1932, as a result of the Lindbergh kidnapping, federal agencies also came onto the case—the FBI's primary jurisdiction was the hostage-taking aspect of the case, while the Bureau of Alcohol, Tobacco, and Firearms was particularly interested in the aspect of weapons violations.

Everyone in Cokeville who had an official responsibility was mobilized. Every EMT and firefighter was suddenly on call. The takeover crisis was the first call for new EMT Glenna Walker, and one of the first for her husband, Kevin, who was already somewhat informed from talking to Princess at the town hall. They had the best reasons for wanting to help: their three children in the school.

The growing official response held an irony few recognized at the time. One reason David had chosen Cokeville, apparently, was that he "didn't want lawmen or others swooping down on him to thwart his plans." But in this part of the sparsely populated, rural West, deadly attacks on one community were quickly seen as attacks against the whole region. Response to the small town's plight was probably as swift and complete as it would have been in a modern, technology-driven, big-city emergency. "Strange he should select a rural area as safer for him than a city metropolis," one observer remarked. "In the latter, he could vanish far more easily into a jungle of buildings and hideouts. Here a helicopter or vehicles could have easily followed him in the wide open spaces."

As the long arm of the law began to curl around Cokeville, word of the takeover began to spread through the town itself. Some fathers pondered whether to unlock big game rifles from their gun cabinets and drive to the school. Some mothers rushed to the police lines set up around the schoolyard; others stayed away, not sure whether their presence would help or hurt. Radio broadcasters Ken Rand of Kemmerer's KMER and Robin Spurling of Afton's KRSV began covering the situation.

High school principal Dale Lamborn had the unpleasant task of notifying students of the intense situation under way. He asked the students to stay away from the hostage scene, even though many had younger brothers and sisters in the building. A number of the high school students were teacher's aides at the elementary school. High school classmates expressed their feelings to each other and especially to fellow students, such as Danny and Billy Mitchell. Their younger brother, Chad, was a hostage. But so were both of their parents, Jack and Jean.

Teacher's aide and high school student Cindy Wixom first learned what had happened when her teacher Richard Pieper, a volunteer fireman, was called out of class. Custodian Bob Dayton came in to sit with the students and explained the matter bluntly: "He's got the kids and he's got the bomb." Cindy's brother Kamron was one of the kids.

Before school dismissed, many of the high school students gathered in the auditorium for a prayer. Dale Lamborn pleaded for divine guidance. Later, students recalled that they and their teachers had been spiritually united as never before. Many wept openly, unashamed to share their deepest feelings of fear and love with classmates and leaders.

"All this and no one even consulted the American Civil Liberties Union," a sophomore remarked.

"Well, the ACLU can go hang its head," another student said. "Those are my friends in there, and I want to do everything possible, and I mean everything possible, to get them out alive."

While the reality of the takeover was being communicated throughout town, in the school building itself, custodian Delbert Rentfro was still trying to figure out what was happening in Room 4. Shortly after Max Excell was on his way to make the first contact with the sheriff's office, Delbert approached the door of the classroom and looked inside. Doris, who was still at the door, apparently decided that Rentfro should be excluded from the hostage group. It is not known why she did this, though it might have been simply the fact that Rentfro, at six feet three inches and 225 pounds, would have been a one hostage they might not be able to control. "Forget it," she said, closing him out almost abruptly. He thought her rude but left for the kitchen, where he had some work to do.

David Young took this time to lay some ground rules. Certain teachers were told to stay away from the area around the door, while Janel Dayton was appointed door monitor. She was instructed to allow no one out. The children were not to use the drinking fountain in the room. "If you drink too much, you'll have to use the bathroom," Young said. And he didn't want them in the bathroom either, even though it was accessible directly from Room 4. *The man does not know children*, Mrs. Dayton thought to herself. *Forbidding nervous children from using a bathroom—how will this ever turn out?*

Doris tried to give the children some practical advice. "Wet some tissue paper and hold it to your face." But this, of course, couldn't work because the children were not allowed to approach the fountain to wet the tissue. Teachers could see that the youngsters were getting confused about what they should and shouldn't do. They turned to combining their efforts in hopes of finding pragmatic solutions to the growing problem. Some handed out nearby books while others asked permission to gather those from farther shelves. David nodded. He seemed to want the children to behave as much as the teachers did.

Eva Clark was still reacting to the reality of being a hostage. With most of her children hostages as well, and the tensions and needs of the immediate situation taking precedence, she had completely forgotten that four-year-old Kathy was still out in the car, waiting for her mother to return from bringing young Paul into school. Eva almost panicked. She approached Doris immediately, trying to explain the problem. "I've got to get out to that car and get my young daughter!" she pleaded.

"You aren't going anywhere," Doris replied.

Eva was desperate. "Please let me go out and get my baby. I'll bring her right in here with me."

Doris clearly wasn't willing to trust that Eva would return. "'You'll stay right here," she repeated with more irritation. She didn't look to David for confirmation; he seemed to know but be disinterested in the outcome.

Eva tried a new approach. "I'll stay here," she agreed. "But can someone else go out and get her?" She suggested Christy or Elizabeth, two of her older children in the room. There was still no positive response. Eva tried one last idea. "How about you getting her then?"

This produced a complete change. Doris immediately said, "Sure, I'll get her," even sounding pleased about the errand. She went out without delay and returned quickly with Kathy, who seemed little ruffled considering her somewhat long and lonely wait.

"The lady was nice to me," she told her mother cheerfully.

Max Excell had returned from his first phone calls and had made his report to David, who accepted what he was told with no display of emotion. Excell was mildly surprised. Before long, David demanded of each teacher a head count of their particular students. He added the figures they gave him so swiftly in his head that the hostages were amazed.

Noting that their students were growing more restless, teachers asked for permission to gather crayons and coloring books and more reading material, anything that might help them keep the children occupied. These requests were granted, with the usual stern warning: "Don't forget to come back, or you know what will happen to the children." When the materials were assembled, teachers realized that they had too few books for the smallest children. They had to ask David for permission to go out again. He was silent, merely gesturing approval. But his eyes told them he had marked in his mind how long they were gone.

Second-grade teacher Carol Petersen helped distribute storybooks and then moved near the door to be with some of her students. She suddenly realized David was watching her closely. She didn't understand why she had caught his attention, but he was definitely studying her. She felt even more exposed when he beckoned her to approach. Perhaps, she thought, she was going to be the first one to die. Why else would he make her stand in front of him? She slowly walked toward him and stopped. But now he was totally ignoring her! She didn't know what to do. Perhaps he had simply wanted her to move away from the door. Quietly, she found a seat somewhere else.

At one point, David made a statement that referred directly to the situation, but not in words that were easy to interpret. He said, in almost a sympathetic tone, "Children are precious. We don't want to hurt them. I'll only shoot the kids with a .22."

With his ground rules announced, David launched into a formal statement of his beliefs. Sitting on a stool, he began, "I'm the most wanted man in this culture. . . . The government and your teachers are polluting your minds. We're going to get some money and. . . ." It was difficult even for those sitting closest to him to hear what he said. They did catch a bit more. "I've got these papers here I've handed to the teachers. They tell you about my philosophy. You will learn later what we have in mind for you." And that was all.

The adults had hoped to keep him talking and say something that would help them understand how to defuse the situation. But he was silent and sullen again. It was about 1:45 p.m.—from then on, Doris did most of the talking. David seemed at times smug and at other times merely bored. He limited his reactions to raising his wrist slightly but ominously if he didn't like something he saw.

Shortly after his speech, David pulled the bomb cart about, not sure where he wanted to place it for maximum surveillance in the 30' × 30' room. Finally, he pulled up a child's desk and leaned on it. This seemed to satisfy him. As he settled down and turned his gaze back on the occupants, his look had the tiresome scrutiny of one obliged to duty.

But to the children, it seemed more malevolent. "He looked mean, as if to keep us frightened," one of the kids said. "And he did."

2:00 p.m.—Jack Mitchell began to notice how difficult it was to breathe. It was more than stuffy in the crowded room—something smelled like gasoline! Jack took a careful look at the bomb cart and realized that the gasoline jug was leaking, albeit slowly. Even as he realized what the problem was, one of the girls got up with a hand over her mouth and ran for the sink. The fumes were clearly making the children sick. Neither Jack nor the girl dared ask David for permission to go to the bathroom. The children were not only frightened of him; now they were becoming ill. Something had to be done.

Jean Mitchell approached David and asked permission to air out the room by opening the windows and doors. David agreed on the condition that a table barricade be set up across the door nearest the bathroom, which was out of his line of sight as he sat facing the center of the room. The windows were too small to become escape routes—the door was his main concern.

The barricade was set up, allowing easy access into the restroom but not beyond into the hallway. Mrs. Dayton was ordered to sit by the door and prevent any child from going through it. At one point she noticed one small boy eyeing the barricade at close range. When he began to climb through, she had to tell him to come back. She hated having to help David keep this youngster imprisoned (see Appendix IX for a drawing of the room).

Opening the windows and doors had made the atmosphere more bearable, but it had also made Doris nervous about the children going near the glass. She alluded to having accomplices at the hallway doors and made hints that snipers were outside, waiting to shoot anyone who got too close to the windows. The children knew these threats could easily be true.

Teachers noted that some of the children were gathered in groups with their heads bowed. "Let's have a prayer. Pass it on," one of Jack Mitchell's sixth graders said. The twelve-year-olds asked Allyson Cornia to voice a prayer for their group. "Father in Heaven, help us. Please help us if the bomb goes off . . ."

"Do you think our Father in Heaven would let us all die?" one boy asked. "No!" said another positively. If David noticed any of these prayers, he said nothing about them. The man who had written that God exists only in man's mind seemed little concerned if the hostages prayed for deliverance.

2:15 p.m.—The children seemed to be having troubles again. Some of those who hadn't shown any fear were now looking shocked and scared. Some moved around aimlessly, looking for something to do and risking becoming a nuisance to David. Some of the children were still reacting creatively, making up mock television scenarios about how they would emerge triumphant. They whispered these to each other when they were far enough away from David. Looking at him only made them frightened again. Several children told Doris that they had headaches. Her solution was simple. "Now listen, children," she told them. "Just don't think about it anymore." That was that.

2:30 p.m.—Jean Mitchell watched the children wriggle with discomfort in the overcrowded room. One child moved a neighbor's leg that had strayed over his own. The owner put it back. There was a small battle of wills with the children frowning at each other. Jean glanced at the man sitting so quietly by his bomb. He was watching the tiff with complete detachment. Jean wondered what would happen when he stopped being detached.

Then she remembered that the dismissal bells would ring in little over an hour. They would signal the children to go home. At 3:25 p.m., would anyone be able to hold them back? Just by instinct, they would try to run out the door, all at once, and then . . .

Her husband, Jack, was talking to the older kids. Like his wife, he had noticed the little ones were having a difficult time. "No one asked for what is happening to us today," he told his sixth graders. "You are the oldest students. We need you to be brave. We all feel fear here, but for a while, we must not show it. I'm counting on you. I know you can do it."

Rocky Moore chimed in, "That's right, kids," he whispered. "I know you can do it too."

The twelve-year-olds thought they were old enough to help. They circulated quietly from one little one to the next, smiling, giving a pat on the back, telling them they would get out of this somehow. Jack and Rocky proudly watched their kids respond to the challenge. It tore Jack up to see them under such stress, no matter how well they were facing it. Suddenly, he felt a surge of energy. He could hold back his feelings no longer. "We've got to get the children out of here! We'll have them out by 4:00 p.m.!"

David's reaction was immediate. He jerked his hand down to the gun in his belt but then stopped. Jack sat down, horrified at what he had almost set off. Jean, just as terrified, saw the anger slowly drain from David's face. Her boy Chad, sitting nearby, gave his mother a fierce hug. She felt both agony and relief in his embrace. Why, why did David have to put the children through this?

As Jack thought about what had just happened, he realized with complete clarity that he and the other teachers were powerless. "There is absolutely nothing any mortal can do," he said to himself. "We are utterly helpless. Even if we stormed the man, he could shoot a child or explode the bomb as he falls down."

Doris approached Jack, carrying something in her hand. She had found an EMT radio in another room, and now she asked him to show her how to use it. Jack, a licensed ham radio operator, knew how but wasn't going to help her. He said he didn't know how to use it. Doris, however, experimented with the dials and managed to find the police channel herself. She was soon listening to every stratagem the authorities were at that moment discussing outside the building. She even heard Patrolman Brad Anderson report to the town hall that he had set up a command post where he could look down the school's south hallway from a Main Street backyard.

Principal Excell was out on one of his telephone contact runs for David. As soon as he returned, Jack quietly motioned him over. "Tell the police to get off the radio! They'll have to communicate some other way. These people can hear everything they're saying outside."

When Excell went out for his next call, he reported the problem. Within a few minutes, the police channel went dead. The small psychological victory gave the teachers fresh hope.

As Excell was on his way to make that call, Delbert Rentfro was on his way back from the kitchen, still uncertain about the goings-on in Room 4. Now he heard the telephone ringing repeatedly with no one answering. As he came down the hall, he saw Excell hurrying toward his office. "Delbert!" exclaimed the principal. "We're all being held hostage in Mrs. Mitchell's room. Get over to the town hall while you can. Tell them to be sure they keep everyone away from the school building! We can't risk anyone trying to get in."

The custodian hurried out of the building, found no one barring his way, and ran to the town hall. There, he relayed his boss's message, giving the lawmen a good description of the Youngs and their location in the school and updating the initial information Princess had given. After giving his report, he suddenly felt strange. He almost wished he was inside that room with the kids. He felt separated and horribly frustrated, not knowing what was happening to them.

Many other people felt as he did. The high school track team, competing at Casper, Wyoming, in a regional meet, was notified of the crisis. "We had no more heart to do anything but finish up quickly and get home," one athlete said.

"Our brothers and sisters were in that school. I think others did as I did. They prayed; then they prayed again," another student commented.

The senior civics class was taking a tour of Utah's Point-of-the-Mountain prison just south of Salt Lake City. One of the students, Andra Birch, remarked that she would "be glad to get back to Cokeville, where I didn't have to think about problems with crime and criminals." When she arrived home, she learned her little brother was one of those being held hostage by a man with an arsenal and a bomb.

2:45 p.m.—Jean quietly flagged her husband's attention. She reminded him about the dismissal bells—they needed to be switched off soon. Jack approached David and asked for permission to leave. David studied him for a minute but voiced no opposition. He didn't concern himself now about anyone returning. They knew the result if they didn't. Jack rushed to Tina's office and easily located the switch. He was back so quickly it seemed too brief for such a vital task. "It's done," he told his wife.

Almost 3:00 p.m.—Teachers and older students watched two of the younger ones quarrel over the "funnest toys." One grabbed another boy's construction block. John Miller was keeping his eyes open for any change in the air. Gloria Mower and media aide Gayle Chadwick were both grateful nothing had happened to trigger the bomb yet, but they wondered how much longer the standoff could go on.

Seven-year-old Jay Metcalf didn't understand what was happening—all this strange talk, the strange man with the strange look and the strange behavior. He felt strange himself. Quiet tears started to roll down his cheeks. Doris handed him a tissue.

Cindy Cowden watched what was going on around her and decided that if she and the children lived, she wanted to work at this school. "I loved these children for their determination to make the best of their circumstances. They wanted to do what their teachers told them. I fell in love with them," Cindy said. Several children near her again began to pray. She held their hands and prayed with them. *They haven't given up hope*, she thought. *Neither can I.*

Suddenly, Jeremiah Moore remembered it was his birthday. David was asked if they could sing "Happy Birthday." Surprisingly, not only did David agree, but he and Doris joined in halfheartedly. Because the music seemed to have a settling influence on the children, David allowed other songs to be sung. Kliss Sparks stood up to lead, and for several precious minutes, some of the smaller children almost forgot where they were and why.

After the sing-along, Jack Mitchell watched as the reinvigorated kids began to wander dangerously close to David and the bomb cart. David even gestured to clear the kids away. From the nearest desk, Jack took some masking tape. Quickly, he taped off what he told the children was a "magic square." The forbidden area left a wide berth around David and his cart. "Don't go across this line!" Jack told the children. "If you do, you're out of the game!" He was relieved to see the gap widen between David and the kids.

Some of the children held an almost congenial conversation with Doris. Drew Cornia wanted to know how long they would be there. When Doris told him ten days or more, he paused. "If you're going to hold us here ten days, I hope you brought us some toothbrushes."

"I hadn't considered that," Doris said with the trace of a smile.

3:05 p.m.—Suddenly, David must have felt too warm. He decided to remove his jacket and sweater, even though it required lifting the same wrist with the shoelace trigger. Everyone in the room held still, mesmerized as they watched David pull his sleeve down to the shoelace-trigger. At one point, he seemed stuck. Doris assisted him, and he finally got the garment peeled down to the wrist, where he let it stay. "I could not hear anyone breathing," Kam Wixom said. "It was as if we had turned to statues. We didn't dare do anything until he quit moving his wrist around."

At times, David seemed to show signs of confusion. At other moments, he still seemed smug. "People pay attention when you're holding elementary school children," he gloated to Excell.

Kliss Sparks also noticed David's erratic behavior. She asked for permission to visit the library again to get more books for the children. It was readily given. "But if you don't come back, one of these kids is going to die," David told her suddenly and sharply. His voice was much more menacing than before.

3:10 p.m.—The children were running out of coloring book pages. Jean asked permission to leave "just to make copies on the machine in the faculty room." David granted permission. But when Jean got there, she realized the machine had been off for two hours and would now take at least four minutes just to warm up. She knelt down and prayed fervently while waiting for the minutes to pass. "We've tried everything! Please help the children do what we cannot do for them." Getting up to make her copies, she felt better for admitting how tense she had become through the endless afternoon.

On returning to Room 4, Jean felt David's eyes on her and knew he had noted the delay. She passed out the papers and tried to get the youngsters involved as quickly and quietly as she could.

During her absence, Jack and student teacher Kris Kasper had been given time to bring a television set from the media center to Room 4. A crowd of children, particularly the little ones, clamored eagerly for cartoons. *Transformers*, a big favorite, came on, and the children watched, engrossed, as the cartoon creatures changed from one form to another, endlessly making war with each other. Travis Walker watched their fascination with the big bangs and shoot-outs on the screen. "Hollywood explosions don't hurt anyone," he said.

3:20 p.m.—For some reason, Travis felt compelled to leave his friends and go across the room to his sisters. After talking with them briefly, he rejoined his pals. Some of the children were beginning to wander aim-lessly about again. David saw them but did not threaten them as before.

3:30 p.m.—Jean Mitchell grew nervous. Had someone warned the bus drivers not to come by? What would the kids do if they heard the buses? Had Excell gotten word to the drivers? She wanted to call to him and ask but didn't dare.

3:35 p.m.—Several teachers sensed the atmosphere begin to change. "Something was about to happen," Jean Mitchell recalled later. "You could feel the unbearable tension mounting."

Eva Clark was aware of the same thing. She looked at the man with the guns and the bomb. His confidence was ebbing! Something strange was occurring—she could feel it, but she couldn't pin down what it was.

3:45 p.m.—Unexpectedly, David called Doris over. He wanted to go to the bathroom. Everyone watched quietly while he changed the shoe-lace-trigger from his wrist to hers. No one had heard him say anything to Doris about the bomb, and he didn't say anything now. Leaving her in his place, David walked past Jean Mitchell toward the bathroom.

Jean knew the room had child-sized fixtures. "You'll just die when you see the inside," she said.

David didn't find the remark amusing. He stepped inside and shut the door.

Once David was out of sight, the children relaxed. But with the removal of the tension he generated, they immediately became more rest-less and noisy as well. "Children!" said Jean Mitchell, "We need quiet time." In the mounting hubbub, she was beginning to feel ill. David had not reappeared and Jean did not want him suddenly walking out into even a semblance of disorder and confusion. Raising her hand to her head, she admitted to Doris, "I've got a headache."

"So do I," said Doris, and she made the same gesture with her hand. It was the hand the trigger was tied to.

In an instant, a huge ball of orange flame cracked into being with a deafening roar from wall to wall. Within a moment, everyone was blinded by choking black smoke. Jean Mitchell felt herself lifted up by the blast wave and thrown toward the door.

The deadman's bomb had blown.

Chapter Four

More than a Miracle

"Labeling it a miracle would be the understatement of the century."
—Richard Haskell, bomb expert

"We're all dead!" Tina Cook cried out as the room exploded around her. Bursting lights snapped out in a wave of searing heat and unbearable pressure.

Eva Clark, tossed from her chair, saw Doris Young, dreadfully illuminated against the pitch-black smoke, engulfed by the fireball she had just unleashed. In the hellish pandemonium, with the clang of fire alarms suddenly beating on her eardrums, Eva felt like she was inside a sonic boom. She had never known fear like this.

Children screamed in pain and panic. Everyone who could run or walk did so, while those who couldn't crawled or blindly groped, searching for air and the closest way out.

"Run!" boomed Jack Mitchell's voice in the half-dark of smoke and burning debris. "Get out of here! *Run!*" Jack knew David Young might still be unharmed, waiting to shoot down the children and adults who had endured the tension better than he.

Janel Dayton struggled to get her bearings. She saw the fire, the smoke, and the chaos surrounding her, yet everything was utterly still. She realized she couldn't hear anything at all. In the silence, she remembered she had been guarding the south barricade, as David Young had ordered. Immediately, she began to dismantle the pile of furniture to clear a path for the children.

The smoke rolled away momentarily, and she looked back into the room. Jean Mitchell was lying on the floor not far away, alive but finding it difficult to move. Janel ran to her aid. She tried to help Jean stand, but neither had enough strength. Suddenly, smoke more thick and acrid than before rolled over them. Janel couldn't breathe. Choking and forced to abandon Jean, she plunged through the south door into the hallway, then up to the other door, hoping to find her first graders.

The deafening explosion seemed to leave Carol Petersen numb. She had been sitting on the floor with kids curled across her lap. When they were swept away by the force of the explosion, she tried to stand, but her muscles wouldn't respond. Terrified, she felt ridiculous as well. Was she going to die here because her legs had fallen asleep?

In the southeast corner, a great shower of flame descended on a large group of kindergartners and first graders who had been intently watching TV. Children screamed in pain and fright as their clothes and hair caught fire. Some tried to escape from the deadly location; others attempted to beat out the flames with their bare hands.

Few knew it at the time, but the design of this deadman's bomb sent most of its explosion thrusting up to the ceiling once the device was set off. From there, the force powered out to the walls and plummeted straight down their sides. Anyone sitting or standing near those walls took the explosion's hottest and heaviest impact.

In contrast, children standing near the border that marked the "magic square" took the first brunt of the detonation. It seemed to Christy Clark that her skin itself was on fire.

Kam Wixom and Travis Walker were luckier. They were near the doorway as the bomb went off and suddenly found themselves thrust into the hallway to safety. Tina Morfeld, farther inside the room, caught a billow of superheated air. Unable to see where to run, she had to take a breath. Instantly, the biting heat scorched her throat and lungs.

Billie Jo Hutchinson was also near the magic square, or "line of death," as the older children secretly dubbed it. Before she could move, she was hit by a wall of fire. Shocked and numbed by the blast, at first she felt no pain. All around her, teachers were probing for bodies, hoping to feel life in the small arms and legs they grasped or hear the muffled call of a child, injured but alive, still strong enough to cry for help.

Rocky Moore was near the windows. Instantly, he grabbed the first kids he saw and began stuffing them through the ten-inch-wide opening of the small ventilation window. He was amazed at how fast they went through. But the children, still dazed—some in shock—were slow to run. "I looked out and saw them stacking up like a cord of firewood," Rocky said. Still not sure whether David Young was nearby, he screamed at the kids, "Run! Run! Get away from the building!" They ran as hard as they could, then suddenly stopped at the edge of the lawn, just as in school fire drill, where they'd been taught to wait for their teachers. Obedient little beggars! Rocky yelled at them again, "Get off the school ground, get out of sight!"

He turned back to look for more kids and was horrified to see blackened faces on some, and others with clothes still glowing. Several ran toward him with their hair in flames. He and the other teachers had no towels or blankets—they could only smother the flames with sleeves and bare hands. He kept the little bodies moving through the window frame—there was no time to check for minor or even serious injuries. First priority was to get them out alive.

By this point, Rocky had only seen children who he knew had been on his side of the room. It was hard to feel any confidence that those closest to the fireball and the acrid smoke had survived. As it was, the smoke would overcome everyone if they didn't all get out soon.

In some ways, the children on the opposite side of the room had an advantage because the doors allowed immediate escape, if only they could find them.

Out in the hallway, Jack Mitchell was looking for his wife. "Have you seen Jean?" he called to a figure running down the hall. He did not know she had been blasted toward the door, that Janel Dayton had tried and failed to help her, or that she had finally been able to half-crawl to safety by herself. The smoke-obscured figure passed him by without a response.

Running took on an almost mystical importance—if you could run, you could live. Kindergartner Johnny King ran into the schoolyard crying, "I don't wanna die!" He finally collapsed at the feet of Judy Himmerich, his aunt.

"I don't know how I got out in the hallway," Kam Wixom said later. "And I don't know why I turned north to those doors. I just found myself running." When he realized he was outside and safe, he yelled, "I'm alive! I'm alive!" At the time, he thought he was running fast, but he explains "I guess my legs were starting to go rubbery. I saw a little first grader tear past me toward Main Street. Being panic-stricken helped him run like I'd never seen him before."

Music teacher John Miller was trying to dismantle the rest of the barricade that Janel Dayton had been working on when she tried to help Jean Mitchell and was nearly overcome by smoke. John was desperate to pull the last chairs and tables apart so the exit was clear.

At that moment, David Young's face appeared at the open restroom door. He was holding a .22 pistol in one hand and a .44 in the other. There was no recognition or reaction in his expression, but John knew, as he looked into David's face, that he was in trouble. Instantly, he turned and ran. At first, there was no place to go. He heard the gunshot and felt it "thud." Not certain he had actually been hit, he found his way outside and began to run. The smoke-free, clear spring air convinced him he was finally safe.

But this euphoria didn't last long. He began to feel more and more dizzy, even as he ran toward Main Street. He collapsed at the edge of Robinson's yard, almost at Janel Dayton's feet. Mrs. Dayton herself was still trying to catch her breath. Kam Wixom ran up just in time to see the EMTs sprint to Miller's aid. Finding blood from a bullet wound below his right shoulder blade, they loaded him in a waiting ambulance and rushed to Bear Lake Memorial Hospital, over the border in Montpelier, Idaho.

Watching near Kam was fellow student Brenda Hartley. Kam was shocked and startled to see her blackened face, but she turned out not to be so much burned as smothered in soot. The plastic decoration on her T-shirt had melted in the heat.

Rocky Moore had finally pushed the last child he could see out the window. Still not sure just what to do, he decided to leave while he could. He took a deep breath and wriggled through the narrow opening, expecting to crash unceremoniously on the ground. Suddenly, he was caught. He felt a spurt of fear, imagining David Young approaching from behind, ready to wrestle him back into the room or shoot him as he tried to escape. Rocky looked back—there was no one—yet something was holding him fast.

Suddenly, he recognized the loud crack of gunshots. Thinking it was David, he battled with panic, trying to get out. But David wasn't there. What sounded like a spray of gunfire was in fact the hundreds of cartridges Young had lined up against the classroom wall. In the soaring temperatures of the burning room, they were starting to explode spontaneously. Feeling along the window frame, Rocky realized he had only been stopped by his belt, which had caught on the protruding window latch. He freed it and tumbled to the grass in a heap. The minutes he was entangled had seemed like hours.

On the far side of the room, Eva Clark had been behind John Miller when she realized her daughter Kathy was not at her side. She had no choice but to grope back into the stifling, acrid, half-blinding conflagration if she wanted to find her youngster alive. But to do so, she also had to pass Doris Young. Eva realized Doris must have taken the bomb's full force. She also knew there was nothing she could do for the woman who was suffering such agonizing pain. Her only duty now was to locate her four-year-old and escape. Poking around the room, she thought she saw a familiar form. Then the little girl reached up. "Mamma!" she cried. Eva pulled her daughter free and pushed toward the exit where her other children were waiting.

There in the doorway was David, still holding a pistol in each hand. Eva knew she was completely defenseless—yet she thought she saw a look of surrender in his eyes that had not been there before. "I will never forget the man's face," she said, recalling the experience later. "It had the look of defeat. . . . His will to continue was shattered." She waited no longer, but turned her back on him, shielding the children, and hurried with them out the door. No gunshot followed their retreat. Soon, they were at the end of the hallway and free.

On the lawn, Rocky Moore had picked himself up and was glancing back through the window. He was amazed to see more youngsters arrive. This time, he pulled them through from the outside, and as he did, he saw someone who lifted his spirits greatly. It was Cindy Cowden, the young woman who was only in Cokeville that day because she wanted to teach elementary school. She had been on the far side of the room, and from her presence, Rocky knew that at least some of those closest to the bomb had survived. Then he saw student teacher Kris Kasper come around the comer of the outside wall—another person who had been in a different part of the room from Rocky. He felt more hopeful that others had survived too.

Substitute teacher Pat Bennion was also at the windows, trying to lift children through. Badly hit by the fire flow down the wall when the bomb went off, she was too busy helping the children climb out to notice that her arms had been seared. The skin was becoming more and more abraded by repeated lifting and pushing across the window frame. She would need expert medical care, and soon.

One of the last to leave Room 4 was Verlene Bennion, the sixty-six-year-old teacher's aide. She suffered second-degree burns on her arms and back and had to be treated for smoke inhalation as well. She remembers feeling a great desire, as she worked her way toward the door, for every person in the room to live at least as long as she had up to that moment.

Once they were safely outside, some of the children living in town ran directly home without even looking to see if their parents were among the crowd milling around the school. Conversely, many parents had left home and come to the police barricade, simply unable to wait passively for news.

Lowell Clark, alerted by his high school daughter, Beverly, was one in the crowd of some two hundred parents gathered outside the school grounds. He had no idea his wife, Eva, was inside the school with their children. Everyone nearby had heard the explosion. The sense of desperation and dread became more and more tangible as the seconds passed. Then Lowell saw and heard bewildered children stream from the school and run toward them, sometimes to the first adult they could recognize, sometimes just to anyone who would wrap them in a safe embrace. Parents found it hard to recognize their own youngsters behind the blackened faces with burned clothes and singed hair that came stumbling up to them.

Lowell was amazed to see Eva leading their children from the school. How had she gotten there? But as he looked over his family with enormous relief and gratitude, his heart stopped. "Where's Christy?" he asked his wife. Eva had no idea. Both of them immediately began asking around in case someone had seen her. Eva was frightened she was back there in that room full of debris and smoke, and possibly David Young. She couldn't bear to think she might have saved five of her children, only to lose the sixth.

Returning teachers were no less agonized by fears that a child might have been left behind. As each of them safely escaped, he or she was besieged by anxious parents, all with the same question: "Where is my child?"

Kliss Sparks could be heard above the general clamor, shouting, "Fourth graders, over here!" Several students volunteered to look for the ones Mrs. Sparks couldn't find.

Jack Mitchell was assembling his sixth graders, while Jean tried to take a mental count of her first graders. Some were still missing.

Several of the Main Street homes that bordered the schoolyard had been evacuated earlier when officials realized how powerful the bomb was. These homes were turned into temporary treatment centers as the EMTs set up triages for the hostages. Those who did not need medical attention telephoned home, trying to find their parents. More often, their parents were already there, searching through the escaping children one by one, trying to be calm as searches sometimes stretched into hours. As the initial shock of the bomb blast and then the frantic escape wore off, students and teachers alike began to feel the extent of the injuries they had received.

From the moment the bomb exploded, EMTs, firemen, and lawmen prepared and then attempted to get inside the building. Principal Excell had been on the telephone, talking to a newspaper reporter at the critical moment. "The bomb's exploded!" he yelled into the telephone, accidentally dropping it. Immediately, he picked it up and called the town hall, repeating the identical message. Sheriff's Deputy Earl Carroll didn't need to be told. Those at the town hall heard the explosion clearly. It was impossible not to imagine the sounds of children screaming.

Excell grabbed his fire extinguisher and ran down the hall, but as soon as he saw the huge cloud of smoke bursting from Room 4, he gave up. Running outside, he saw law officers running toward him. Excell yelled at them to hurry. "I can hear ammo exploding," he said. "They must be shooting the children!"

While some of the officers were trying to get into Room 4, others were frantically trying to keep citizens from overrunning the building. Parents broke from the police cordon toward school entrances in a wall of anxiety. One father ran forward, cursing loudly. "I'm going in there after that SOB myself," he yelled. Police officers begged townspeople to stay back so that EMTs and firemen could get through.

Patrolman Brad Anderson knew he had to get in quickly. If David Young was there and still armed, he could be shooting randomly, just to take as many with him as possible. Anderson knew that half the problem would be the room itself—in the fiery and smoky aftermath, it would be just as easy to mistake a teacher or older student for Young as it would be to let David slip by, thinking he was one of them. Anderson wanted to prevent either of those things from happening.

He checked his bulletproof vest and drew his service revolver. Sheriff's Deputy Greg Goodman joined him, and the two stepped through the double doors into the school. Their first encounter was with a shadowy figure who fit the general description of David Young but who turned out to be the father who had been threatening to "go get" David Young. How he had gotten inside they couldn't be sure, but he was ordered out immediately and told he was lucky to be alive. His son, it turned out, was already on the way home—despite his ordeal—pedaling there on his own bike.

Patrolman Anderson didn't know that Police Chief Cal Fredrickson had returned and come directly to the school, still in his civilian clothes. He was already in the building but coming from a different direction, moving toward the other two. Deputy Goodman, who lived in Kemmerer, didn't know Chief Fredrickson well, and the two men drew their pistols on each other as their paths converged. A second deadly accident was narrowly avoided as Anderson identified the men to each other.

Anderson and Goodman were now able to move toward Room 4. Reaching it, Anderson opened the door while Goodman propped a chair against it. Brad had already decided that rushing into the center of the room would be wiser than peering around the corner of the door. The gunman would be seeing them against clear daylight, where they would only be viewing an atmosphere the consistency of pea soup.

Just as they opened the door, the men heard a gunshot. Before they could react, layers of thick, oily smoke poured out. Anderson, unable to locate an air pack before going in, had never found breathing so difficult. The fumes were both piercing and unavoidable. He moved back, followed by Goodman, and the two men pondered their next move. Then, from inside the room came a second shot. The door spring, which had begun pushing at the chair, forced it away completely. The door slammed shut.

Despite their need to get inside, both men decided to wait at least briefly for the smoke to clear. While they waited, someone at the far end of the hallway turned off the alarm bell. Earl Carroll had located the proper key. As they recovered their ability to breathe normally, Anderson and Goodman talked quietly, keeping a wary eye on both ends of the corridor. Suddenly, a voice boomed down the hallway. "We've found one subject dead in the bathroom!"

Sheriff's Deputy Randy White had located an air pack and gotten safe access to Room 4 just before Anderson and Goodman arrived. He could see no one moving about, so he approached the restroom door cautiously and pushed it open a crack. When this produced no response, he carefully peeked around the door. A man's body was slumped with its leg pressed against the doorway. This must be David Young.

Chapter Five

Personal Impacts

This is the kind of entry no one—not in her wildest imaginations—figures she would make in a journal. . . . Our son is one of the hostages." This was my wife's journal entry May 18, 1986, two days after the bomb went off.

On the day of the event, our high school-aged daughter, Jenny, had run frantically into the house from the bus stop. Sobbing and calling almost hysterically to her mother, she gave the terrifying news.

"Did you hear? Don't you know what's happened?" Jenny cried. She and her best friend, Carrie Anderson, were confused and grief-stricken. Their faces displayed the stunned disbelief they felt. "Some people with bombs are holding the elementary school hostage! They're going to hold them for ten days!"

"My mind went blank," wrote my wife, Judene, in her journal. "I was annoyed with the girls for going too far with one of their pranks. This was, well, just too absurd! They're full of pranks, but their grief was all too real. I had to believe them, yet I was numb with disbelief.

"I sat down with them, trying to comfort them while at the same time trying to sort this out in my head. Nothing sorted.

"I felt so . . . alone, confused, frustrated. In desperation, I fell on my knees and pleaded for help that the children would somehow find the courage they needed to withstand this ordeal. I felt relief—I was afraid to feel assured," the journal entry concluded.

I hadn't seen my wife in five days. For the first time, I had commuted home early for the weekend from Provo, Utah, where I was working as advisor to the student newspaper at Brigham Young University.

The only hint I had of anything wrong came as I approached Cokeville and headed toward my home about six miles north of town. A normally conservative neighbor sped past me going about eight miles per hour in a sixty-five mile per hour zone. I thought I noted a worried look on his face, but figured it was just a personal matter. Instinctively, I checked my own speedometer and continued driving. It seemed like a peaceful afternoon. There was no particular reason to hurry.

From home, Judene had just watched two ambulances and a police car speed past on the highway heading for town. As I turned down our driveway, she was conversing with Cindy Dayton, who had been a substitute teacher at the high school that day. Her tear-streaked face showed her desperate desire to just "wake up from this whole thing."

Spotting me, my wife came running up the driveway. As she threw herself into my embrace with more intensity than ever before, I first thought this was an extra special kind of a greeting. But seeing her face filled with anguish kept me from enjoying the moment.

"Is everything all right?" I asked, looking into her eyes.

"No! The grade-school kids are being held hostage by someone with a bomb. . . . They want millions of dollars. They have guns. . . ." The scenario gushed out in a flood.

"What?" I found myself saying.

"Our son is in there!"

When my wife told me that, I first envisioned an idle threat, a fake bomb. Passersby who maybe had too much to drink.

My mind turned to the practical; we would need to take sleeping bags and several days' food to wait at the schoolyard entrance, no matter how long it took. If the extortionists took a child to make their getaway . . . well, it would complicate everyone getting out of this unharmed.

It would do no good to speculate. We needed more details about this dilemma.

The two of us were joined by another high school-age daughter, Cindy, and Joanne Metcalfe, a neighbor who had three children in the classroom. The two mothers shared a hug; it was the only way to express the feelings words couldn't. Joanne's husband, Jack, had taken his high school civics class on a field trip. Knowing she needed support from someone in this grotesque circumstance, we invited her to come inside the house.

Joanne called the school. When Principal Max Excell answered, Joanne quickly blurted out, "What's going on there?"

"It's true! There's a man here with a bomb. I can't tell you much more—I've got to go."

None of us had any idea at the time how much pressure Excell was under to make every moment count.

In our living room, there was heavy silence mixed with confusion as we attempted not to assume the worst. Then, Joanne's high school-aged son, Aaron, burst into our living room. "The bomb went off! *Boom!* I just heard on the radio!"

The two families headed toward town in separate vehicles. I thought of Kam's smile the week before as he showed me his tree hut, his proud look when he brought in a gallon of milk from the dairy barn on a subzero morning, the last picture he had drawn of a "super car of the future." The future. . . .

I also thought of the children now being held hostage, the ones I had taught in the Honors English class mid-year. These fifth and sixth graders put out their own newspaper, "wondering what we can use for exciting news." Several of the students had also enthusiastically created stories that might have been published in magazines elsewhere. One was a detective story about children in a small town being kidnapped. *What a wonderful imagination*, I had thought. The teachers—I had worked with them daily. My wife and I saw them frequently in almost every community activity. What was happening to them?

Probably every vehicle hurrying to the school grounds held people with similar thoughts. Many talked openly and freely of their anxiety to find out more, and when they did, all spoke of their feelings of helplessness. Most said unashamed prayers on behalf of the hostages and their families.

As I parked my car at the curb just outside the school grounds, I saw Dr. Allen Lowe, Lincoln County School District Superintendent, step from his vehicle. His face was ashen. Few words could be found. A voice on the radio came through the silence—something about parents searching for their children. Here in front of me, I saw it happening.

Children stood dazed on the schoolhouse lawn or nearby homes with the look of incredulity at being alive. Quilts and blankets were hastily gathered from nearby homes. They were being wrapped compassionately and carefully around shivering youngsters, many of whom were waiting for a turn at oxygen tanks. There were ambulances everywhere, from everywhere. Children in some families were taken to hospitals in five different communities: Montpelier, Idaho; Afton, Kemmerer, and Evanston, Wyoming; and Logan, Utah. Some were later taken to a Salt Lake City burn center.

Several children with blackened faces and arms were coughing from the effects of smoke inhalation.

It struck us immediately that though this was an unbelievable event, all of the chaos was somehow transforming into precise organization. If some fathers, as was rumored, were carrying deer rifles, there were none now to be seen. Everyone was functioning in his or her own field of expertise. We recognized EMTs Kevin and Glenna Walker, who had three children in the smoke-filled building. Teenagers were handing out cups of water.

Even though paramedics came from different counties and nearby states, they were working as if coordinating a drill. Many frantic faces wore the same wide-eyed expression. For most, the horror of the event had not yet been fully realized, nor would it be for some time yet.

My wife and I jumped out of the car and ran toward the center of activity. Looking through the frenzied crowd, I saw Kamron. He had been calling us from the Taylors' home on Main Street. It must have been an extremely lonely feeling for him to get no answer. He knew his mother would be worrying. His face showed no signs of burns. Just the blankness of shock. Feelings and reality had not yet meshed together.

I raised my hand and called to him. He said I loomed out of the crowd "like a telephone pole." His eyes could see nothing else but his parents, and he came running. He reached his mother first. There were no words. Just an ecstatic embrace.

Later, mother and son looked at a photograph of that memorable reunion. The picture, taken by a television photographer, captured the elation and relief of the moment. It was circulated on network broadcasts and picked up by a wire service. The look on their faces so effectively told the story of this drama taking place that it ran in several newspapers across the country.

Chapter Six

Angels Intervene

Upon finding David Young's body slumped on the floor in the bathroom, Sheriff's Deputy Randy White took the precaution of placing his handcuffs around the man's wrists. He also removed the weapons in the bathroom, including those on David's body. Beyond that, he disturbed nothing, knowing the medical examiner would need the site intact.

Randy's next responsibility was to look for other bodies, a task he dreaded. "I had read many reports of children hiding in fear in out-of-the-way places following fires and explosions. Other lawmen and I now began searching all the little hiding places," he reported.

Chief Fredrickson and Earl Carroll had not heard Randy White call out and were thus searching the building in case David Young was holed up somewhere else. Word was passed to Principal Excell outside that the building was secure. One critical phase of the day's work was over.

Firefighters and EMTs had also been trying to get to the schoolroom, knowing that there still might be people inside who could be saved if the fire and smoke were controlled. As the firemen hooked up their hoses, EMT Kevin Walker thought he heard two shots. Hoses were directed at the windows, but it was soon clear that too little water was getting into the room. Still not knowing whether it was safe to approach the windows, one of the EMTs moved to the larger section above and discovered it didn't open. Barely hesitating, he located a piece of metal pipe and broke the glass, wrestling out the steel frame with his bare hands. Now the firemen could get the water where it was needed.

As they manned the hoses, they thought they saw an adult woman's body on the floor near the far wall. As first it appeared she might be overcome with smoke inhalation. One of the EMTs thought she might still be saved with mouth-to-mouth resuscitation. "But we soon realized the futility," Kevin Walker said. "Air being breathed in was escaping through a hole in her head." The whole top of her skull was missing.

Fireman Allen Burton feared it was his sister, kindergarten teacher Kim Kasper. To make identification easier, the woman's body was pulled through the window and carried on a blanket to the lawn. Adult hostages were asked to look at the body to help make identification certain. All agreed. "That's the woman who was holding us hostage," they told investigators. Though badly burned, her face was still recognizable.

While the crucial identifications of David and Doris Young were being made—allowing lawmen to verify that the crisis was officially over—Lowell and Eva Clark were still searching frantically for Christy. They had split up to cover more territory and were now wondering if police would let them into the school to search for her personally. Before trying to get that permission, however, Eva was approached by a friend who had been entrusted with a message for her: Lowell had found their daughter alive. She was burned—he didn't know how badly—and was being taken by ambulance to Star Valley Hospital in Afton, Wyoming, fifty miles away. Lowell had located her just in time to ride along. Greatly relieved, Eva quickly arranged to leave for Afton herself.

While the hostages had by far the more serious injuries—Deputy Ron Hartley, for instance, learned that all four of his grade-school children had been taken to Bear Lake Memorial Hospital in Montpelier—those assigned to search and restore order also suffered from the experience. One of the lawmen was hospitalized for smoke inhalation. Patrolman Anderson was treated for nearly an hour on the grounds of the school for the same problem. As the crisis phase passed and the search and recovery phase moved forward, parents continued to look for missing children, slowly sorting out who had been taken to which hospital and why.

Two of the most badly burned, Billie Jo Hutchinson and Tina Morfeld, were rushed to expert care immediately. In time, seventy-nine of the hostages were hospitalized and the most critical were transferred to the University of Utah Burn Center in Salt Lake City.

Normal human error occasionally crept in, making already tense and hurting people dig even deeper for patience and stamina. Colleen King, already at the hospital in Montpelier visiting her sick father, was told to stand by: her sons had been burned from a bomb explosion at their school in Cokeville and were on their way to the hospital. Only after waiting an hour and half for them to arrive did Colleen learn that Montpelier was the wrong destination—they had been taken to the hospital in Kemmerer.

While the hostages were being identified and treated, as swiftly and carefully as their situations permitted, everyone still had their minds on what the lawmen and investigators were finding in Room 4. The only question of any importance was who was still inside.

As lawmen, firemen, and EMTs picked through the room rubble, their minds were on this question. The first impression was that of total shambles. While the walls were still upright, much of the ceiling tile had blown out. Debris was everywhere, and everything was black, except for one white patch on the east wall about the size of a human figure with its arms partially outstretched. In the smoke-stained wreckage, this area stood out sharply. It was speculated that the blast had spent its force on some person, most likely Doris Young, leaving the wall area behind that person unseared. But Doris had been in the center of the room. The mystery remained unsolved.

As they worked, searchers continued to be amazed at the destruction in the room. The estimated property damage was later placed at $50,000. With so much destroyed, how had anyone escaped alive, let alone the number of people who did?

Patrolman Anderson kept his mind focused on the task, moving slowly and methodically through everything on the floor. Yet every backpack or abandoned jacket made his heart jump. Was he coming now to the body of a child?

Finally, the lawmen and their cosearchers turned over the last bit of flotsam, examined next to and under the last bit of broken furniture large enough to shield a body, and investigated the far reaches of the last closet. Only then did they dare believe the unbelievable—there were no bodies in the room. Every one of the hostages had gotten out alive.

The good news raced through town, turning what had been dreadful hours of pressure and uncertainty into relief, gratitude, and tears, all to be shared with neighbors and friends, more than likely in the same position themselves. The official investigation was barely underway, but lawmen could now turn to the work ahead with confidence in their professionalism without the fury and pain they expected to feel as soon as they heard the bomb explode.

Their first task was getting rid of the leftover ammunition. The cartridges had already spent themselves by exploding in the heat of the fire inside Room 4. Some of the blasting caps, however, had not detonated, and these were quickly taken care of in specially designed bomb-disposal canisters in a nearby field. David's arsenal of rifles and other guns, no longer a threat to anyone, was taken into evidence.

Whatever remained of the bomb was the next object of investigation. Explosives expert Richard Haskell from Rock Springs, Wyoming, was put in charge. A member of the Sweetwater County Sheriff's Office, he had become familiar with bomb design during military service and during his years as a lawman. The deadman's bomb used by David Young was a familiar type.

As he dismantled the remains of the device, however, Richard found something strange. The two wires that were to detonate two blasting caps and fill the air with exploding gunpowder, were severed, cut cleanly as if snipped with wire cutters. When the battery current could not reach these two caps, there was no power to spray their contents into the room, particularly the aluminum dust, which was supposed to increase the incendiary potential of the air when the bomb went off.

Further, Haskell found that leakage in the plastic jug David used to contain the gasoline component of the bomb had created a partial paste of the granules that were supposed to become airborne at detonation. The bomb had been designed to kill everyone in the room, Haskell concluded, but in those two ways alone it had been prevented from working as David intended. Had the blast occurred as David originally designed it, Haskell said, it "would have caused an explosion caving in the walls and blowing up everything in the room."

In time, official investigations would reveal more unusual aspects to the entire incident, but at the moment, it was the children who began to make statements their parents found remarkable, to say the least.

Seven-year-old Katie Walker told her fourteen-year-old brother, Shane, the first family member she saw after running from the explosion, "They saved us. I said a prayer, and they saved us!"

"Who saved you?" Shane asked.

"The angels," she replied.

Katie saw her mother, Glenna Walker, the recently certified EMT, a few minutes later. "Mommy," Katie repeated, "the angels saved us!"

Glenna patted her daughter on the head. "Yes, we all have much to be grateful for, dear," she said, holding her close.

Glenna did not realize that her daughter wanted to be taken literally. Even though Katie's sister, Rachel, was being treated for burns at the hospital, Rachel and Katie and Travis had all come through their ordeal alive and Glenna hoped they would soon no longer need to talk about the takeover. The children, however, wanted to talk about it.

Dr. Vern Cox was one of the psychologists brought in to help the town work through the fears and feelings generated by David Young's attack. Along with other families in Cokeville, Kevin and Glenna joined the group and individual discussions intended to provide this help. At one of these meetings, Katie and Rachel told Dr. Cox that they had tried to talk with their parents about the angels who had saved them. Their brother Travis also had something serious on his mind. Dr. Cox told their parents what the children had been telling him.

"Why haven't they been telling us, their own parents?" Glenna asked.

"Have you been listening to them?" he asked her. "Really listening?"

Glenna realized that perhaps they hadn't. She and Kevin arranged a time when the whole family could talk.

"They were standing there above us," Katie began. "There was a mother and a father and a lady holding a tiny baby, and a little girl with long hair. There was a family of people. The woman told us the bomb was going off soon and to listen to our brother. He was going to come over and tell us what to do."

"She said to be sure we did what he told us," Rachel added.

"They were all dressed in white, bright like a light bulb but brighter around the face," Katie told her mother.

"The girl had a long dress," Rachel nodded, "which covered her feet, and she had light brown hair." The two girls spoke quietly but firmly about people who had certainly not been among the hostage group in Room 4. There was no apology or self-consciousness. The people they described seemed as real to them as their own parents, who were listening attentively now. Rachel remembered something else—that the figures dressed in white standing above them had moved around to another part of the room just before the bomb went off.

Some time later, my wife and I met with the Walkers to ask them about their roles as EMTs during the hostage crisis. At that visit, their children's unique comments were mentioned. We asked permission to discuss their experiences with them. Glenna and Kevin were understandably reluctant to subject their children to the scrutiny of others about something personal and sacred, even if those people knew and cared about them. But Katie had a different idea. "The woman made me feel good. I knew she loved me. I want to talk about it." Rachel and Travis agreed.

Accordingly, on December 28, 1986, we went to the Walkers, taking our son Kamron and daughter Cindy with us. After the children played together for a while, we asked Travis what he had seen and whether he could describe it to us. "I didn't see anything—nothing," he emphasized. "I just heard a voice. It told me to find my little sisters and take them over by the window and keep them there. I did what I was told. I looked around and found them and told them to follow me over by the window."

He seemed absorbed. I had known Travis for five years and had never seen him look that serious before. "I told them to stay there and not move," he said.

"Did they respond?" I asked.

"They were playing with their friends, and I didn't think they would want to leave them. I knew they had to come with me. They got their coloring pages and I took them over by the windows."

"Did they stay right there?" my wife asked.

Both girls quickly said "Yes."

"But," Travis continued, "I didn't stay there with them. I was also told to help them through the window when the bomb went off. And I went back over with the other boys where I had been, by the door—"

Glenna interrupted and explained that Travis had told Dr. Cox earlier "how terribly guilty he felt—that he had not been by the windows with his sisters when the bomb exploded." There was a long silence.

"I should have gone over by the window with my sisters. That's what I was told to do. I didn't do it."

Glenna told us there was no consolation for Travis in the weeks following the hostage crisis. He did not sleep well for a while, she said. "I have never seen him so upset."

The girls seemed content to discuss their experience at length. They remembered details vividly. Referring to the people they had seen, they were asked, "How did they come into the room? Was it through the main door or the door by the bathroom?"

"Through the ceiling," both girls said at once.

"Where were they standing?"

Katie held her hand about two feet off the ground, just below her waist. "They were about this high off the ground."

"Could you see all of them, their entire bodies?"

Rachel nodded, then said, as though deep in thought, "Except for the little girl. She had a long white dress. I couldn't see her feet."

"Was there any color at all in the clothing they wore?"

Rachel shook her head. "They were all dressed in white."

Kevin suggested looking at some old photos of family members, both living and deceased. Katie did not require a lengthy look as she picked up an old picture in a locket. She didn't talk for a moment, but studied it as if enjoying a happy memory. Then, "She looked like this, only she didn't wear glasses."

Rachel, who had been out of the room briefly, came back in and looked at the photo herself. "That's the angel! But without the glasses," she said emphatically.

Shirley Ruth Thornock, the woman in the picture, was Glenna's mother, who had died when Glenna was only sixteen. "My mother never lived to know my family," Glenna said.

Another photo, this one of Kevin's brother who died in 1961, "looked like" the man who was with the "family of angels," the girls said. But they hadn't looked at him that day as closely as the woman who was doing the talking. They couldn't be sure. There was no explanation for the others mentioned in the group. The girls had never seen nor known any of the others they described, including the little girl with the long brown hair.

I had to ask the traditional question: "Did they have wings?"

"No!" the two girls said without hesitation. "They looked like we do, but all dressed in white," Rachel said.

"Did she smile at you?" I asked, referring to the "angel mother."

Katie pondered the question. "She sort of smiled at me with her voice."

"Did she make you feel you were going to be safe?"

"She said we would be," Rachel replied, "if we did what our brother told us."

We turned to Travis. "Travis, did you feel that you would be protected when the bomb went off?"

"I knew, somehow, we would be if I followed directions. When I heard the explosion, I just forgot about part of what I was supposed to do. I was so close to the hallway, it was easy to get out there. . . . It was a minute later when I thought about my sisters."

"Were all the angels there when the bomb went off?" Kevin asked his daughters.

"I don't know," Rachel replied. "The smoke from the bomb covered them up."

It was getting close to the little girls' bedtime. We had talked together for more than an hour on a subject both sensitive and unusual.

The Walkers expressed their own feelings about what their children had reported. Glenna said, "The children know it happened, and they want to share it. They feel they have a responsibility to share it so others can benefit from it. What others do with their experiences or feelings is up to them."

Kevin pointed out, "It was the children's decision. They stand behind it. We stand behind them. Where would we be—where would any of us be—without the courage to testify of such a spiritual happening?"

Other children, apart from the Walker three, spoke of "messengers" who appeared to them as well. Some families decided it was too personal a matter to put on record. One mother said some people would not comprehend what the children were saying or know what to do with the information. Several other parents said their children gave specific details of someone they didn't know appearing to them in the hostage room. These families specifically requested that their names not be used.

One child who was willing to share his spiritual experience in surviving the takeover was six-year-old Nathan Hartley. Nathan was sitting near the taped line before the bomb detonated. He told his father, veteran sheriff's investigator Ron Hartley, what he saw.

"The lady helped me get out alive," he reported.

"I've been through it all with hours of interrogating suspects and prisoners," Hartley said. "I'm especially trained to detect lying or manipulative answers for personal gain. I asked some more questions."

The first grader continued, "A lady told me the bomb was going to go off very soon. She told me how to save myself. She said to go over by the window, then hurry out when I heard the bomb explode. She told me that I would make it if I did exactly what she said." Nathan said he had never seen the woman before.

As the Walkers had, Ron Hartley leafed through the family album with his son. At one page, Nathan stopped his father. "That's her," he explained abruptly. It was a picture of Flossie Elliott, Nathan's great-grandmother. She had been dead for three years.

In January 1987, Nathan drew a picture of the way it had been. It shows a bright angel over the head of Doris. The stick figures in front represent the students—he didn't see an angel over David's head (see Appendix IX for the drawing). Did the Hartleys feel any concern about relating their son's unique experience? "It happened," Mrs. Hartley said. "I'd rather face people now than explain, either here or in the next life, why we didn't say something about it," she emphasized. "We can't back down from personal convictions."

Three weeks after the takeover, Nathan wrote down specifics of his experience. "Just before the bombs went off," he wrote, "angels came down through the ceiling. They were bright like light bulbs. There were about ten of them holding hands around the children to protect them." One of the angels "told me the bomb was going to go off. . . . All the angels told us to run to the windows when the bomb went off. I was just getting ready to run to the window when it went off."

Later, he wrote, "What I saw was that there were robe-clad people by almost everyone. I looked around and saw that some were floating in the air. I suddenly realized that these people were angels. I looked toward the taped square and saw an angel high above Doris Young. It seemed as if the angel were about to leave."

Years later, when asked about the unique vision, he described it as a "special and sacred experience. . . . For those who want to be benefited by it, that is what happened."

Eva Clark was intrigued with the sensations she had felt while a prisoner of David Young. "I was scared," she said with no reservations. "I was really scared. He had made sure we adults understood that he would not hesitate to shoot us. I was sure we were going to die. For about an hour and a half, time seemed to drag by, if not stand still altogether. But the last hour or so, after praying over and over, [I felt] entirely different. I felt peace. I knew we would make it."

Eva also spoke feelingly of the statements made by the children. "Everyone involved in the investigation of David Young's bomb knows something strange and unexplainable happened. No one has any plausible idea at all how the children safely escaped. I think it is time to listen to them, the hostage children themselves, and let them tell us the reason they all survived. We can label it 'divine intervention' or whatever we want. Whatever we call it, many of these explanations from the children help everything fit together better."

Two other adults found themselves greatly affected by their hostage experience: Rocky Moore and Jack Mitchell. Moore had long joked that he would believe in a God only when he saw his personal "burning bush." He had used the expression every time he needed to avoid a discussion of spiritual things. Now, he wanted to talk about spiritual things. At a high school football game that took place several months after the crisis, someone asked Rocky, "What was it that saved you from the bomb?"

"I'll tell you what happened," he told his questioner. "God was looking out for His kids."

"And you were saved because you were with them?" a bystander asked.

"Exactly," Rocky replied.

"Did you see your burning bush, Rocky?" a child who had been one of the hostages asked.

"You bet I did!" the teacher nearly shouted. "That's enough for me or anybody. And don't you forget it!"

After falling from the classroom escape window, Rocky carried his sprained arm around in a sling. Once mended, he seemed as feisty as ever but almost contentedly ecstatic with memories of the experience. "I don't see," he said at one point, "how there could be any more atheists left in this country."

His former fellow agnostic Jack Mitchell made his change of heart unmistakably clear. In a statement repeated in three different interviews made over several weeks' time, he stated, "I know this; there is no other explanation for what happened. It was divine intervention. A higher power stepped in. We could do nothing for ourselves. There were prayers answered in there. I'll never doubt the power of prayer again."

It would perhaps be easy to discount the hostage children's accounts because of their age, their willingness to please, or their need to make sense of a terrible ordeal by investing it with some eternal significance. It would be equally easy to discount their parents' support because parents are not sufficiently objective to properly judge, or because it's not always possible to determine whether your children are a bit confused, innocently playacting, or actually telling noncollusive lies. And it might be easy to discount sheriff's investigator Hartley's professional approach to his son's reported experience because, just by being the boy's father, his detachment might be questioned.

But the evidence of bomb expert Richard Haskell would also have to be discounted. And he concluded that the explanation for the discrepancy between the impact of the bomb—had it gone off as David designed it—and the effect the bomb actually had, is not to be found in science. His investigations pointed out fourteen factors that unexpectedly minimized the impact of the blast on the hostages, the first of which is the unexplained fact that the blasting cap connecting wires were cut straight through, despite there being no opportunity for that to have happened during the takeover (See Appendix VI for a complete list of the fourteen factors.)

Haskell issued this statement: "I don't know how the wires were cut. My only official conclusion is that I can't begin to explain it." At one time, he said to television reporters, "The whole thing just appears to be a miracle." Asked later about his use of the word "miracle," Haskell not only stood by his statement but also underscored it. "To be more specific," he said, "labeling it a miracle is the understatement of the century."

Chapter Seven

Probing for Answers

"David and Doris Young could have each received a minimum of 3,080 years in prison for the kidnapping charges alone."
—Richard Leonard, Lincoln County attorney

Several days following May 16, 1986, a strange lull seemed to settle upon the community of Cokeville. Many were trying to recover from physical burns and the emotional trauma. Few wanted to talk about it in public. Some of the surviving faculty said they were still trying to put the day's event into perspective. Unfortunately, some were having a difficult time doing it. But fortunately, they were alive! While the perpetrators died, all hostages had been saved.

In this, yes, their many prayers had been answered. In addition, with the intruders dead, none of the children would have to face their captors in a court of law to testify against the man with the evil, terrible eyes. But understandably, some wanted to just forget about anything and everything to do with David Young. The whole ordeal was too painful.

Yet, for law enforcement officials, their work was just beginning. Reports of the tragedy—or was it a triumph?—had to be assessed and sifted, fact from fiction. The *Salt Lake Tribune* carried a headline saying "Aftermath of Explosion 'a Miracle.'" Salt Lake City TV station KUTV did such an excellent job of early coverage that their reports were picked up by a London TV network. Stuart Wilson, a resident in London who had lived in Utah, was startled to see news of a town he knew. KUTV had been so timely, in fact, that their arrival on the scene minutes before the bomb went off evoked semi-serious jokes about "being notified by the Youngs in advance." Part of the legal investigation centered for a time on whether David Young had given someone in the press notification so he could air his political views.

What really happened was that KUTV had a crew in the tri-state area on another assignment. They did not have their portable relay equipment along, but they managed to get footage of children at the moment of their escape, embracing parents in a reunion that was the envy of every other television station. Photos were put on the wire and picked up by numerous newspapers around the nation.

With a variety of news outlets on the scene in the next week, a scramble for an "angle" was more the focus than was accuracy. In describing the initial phase of the takeover, an article in *Time* magazine had over thirty errors or distortions.

Fortunately, there also was press coverage both sensitive to the feelings of people in the town and accurate to the story itself. Here are a few "sound bite" examples from different media organizations:

Carol Mikita, KSL_TV, Salt Lake City: "It is a story of tragedy and twisted thinking."

Greg Lefevere, CNN, Atlanta: "A town of miracles? That could be right. A third of the town was being held hostage . . . strong family ties pulled them through."

Charlene Brown, KUTV, quoting one of the hostage schoolgirls, referring to Doris and David Young: "She was a nice lady, but the guy sounded like he was going to kill everybody."

Bomb expert Richard Haskell, interviewed on CNN: "The false ceiling absorbed much of the bomb blast. I can't express how fortunate they are. It's unreal . . . so fortunate. You look in there and wonder why there aren't 150 kids lying in there dead."

One article perceived by the eyewitnesses as particularly error-free was that published in *U.S. News* and *World Report*, which came out about two weeks after the incident. The article contained the photograph of a small child peering into the schoolroom that had been the scene of terror several days before. The caption read: "Inch by Inch." Both article and picture received high acclaim from hostages and eyewitnesses to the incident, who felt it captured not only the facts of the story but the poignancy as well.

One of the first to fully comprehend the significance of David Young's diaries was the Salt Lake City *Deseret Morning News.* In a story dated May 31 (thirteen days after the fact, which gave them sufficient time to research the accuracy of their statements) the newspaper said, "Investigators now believe the 'Biggie' was much bigger—and more horrible—than at first suspected. Young's writings indicated he was planning on '. . . a place where he could rule as God of a new race, a place that could only be reached through death.' The ramifications are . . . terrible."

The best story about the press itself was probably that running in Wyoming's *Star Valley Independent,* written by Cokeville correspondent Gwen Petersen. The headline was "Cokeville bombed with news media." The article ran,

> It's been a new experience for most of the people of Cokeville to be so closely associated with the news media. Television cameras were on the scene shortly after the bombing tragedy occurred and have stayed throughout the week. A satellite truck transmitting live coverage has parked near the elementary school, and anyone walking down the street has been subject to an interview. Residents opened their homes to newsmen, providing telephone service for calls all over the country. Principal Max Excell received calls from San Francisco radio stations and the *Sunday Today* newspaper from London, and he was interviewed by the UPI wire services out of Washington, and countless others who were on the scene. The incident has received excellent coverage from the media. The people of Cokeville are now looking forward to the time when the news people will leave so they can go on with their lives.

Within fifteen minutes after the bomb exploded in Cokeville, Lincoln County's Assistant Attorney Richard Leonard was at the schoolhouse to provide legal advice, including questions of proper search warrant and investigative procedure. He would initiate the monumental criminal investigation. The takeover, in Leonard's own words, "appeared to us to be the most extensive act of terrorism ever attempted in the United States [at that time]."

Leonard was prepared to charge both David and Doris with kidnapping, had they lived. If convicted of that crime alone, each could have received a minimum of twenty years for each of the 154 hostages. That would have added up to 3,080 years apiece. While the plan was David's, Doris was clearly complicit. She entered the school building on her own volition, without any known coercion from her husband. Add to that the penalty for extortion, and the Youngs would have needed all the years they dreamed of in their Brave New World just to serve out their sentences! Further, had David lived, there would have been the added crime of murder for shooting his wife. (An investigation concluded that David had shot his wife after she caught fire from the explosion.)

The authorities felt that Princess would probably not have been charged, possibly even if she had remained in the school with her father, due to the fact that her life was often threatened.

Along with Leonard, Lincoln County sheriff's investigators Earl Carroll and Ron Hartley spent days in the schoolroom, talked to hostages, and pored over evidence in the case. All were veterans at their jobs. Leonard had spent more than five years in the attorney's office, while Carroll had been a police chief in Utah for twelve years before joining Lincoln County. Hartley had also spent years with the county as an investigative officer. Together, they launched a thorough probe into everything known about David and Doris Young: their possessions, travels, lifestyle, and particularly their diaries.

When Hartley arrived in Cokeville, he had heard nothing on his car radio of the crisis and assumed a "massive mock drill" was in progress. He was soon told otherwise and taken inside the school building. Later, the forty-one diaries and journals of David and Doris that had been located were turned over to Hartley, who began the complicated process of examining them, both for a basic understanding of the two personalities and for specific references to "the Biggie" of May 16, 1986.

While the takeover was underway (but prior to the explosion), two agents from the Federal Bureau of Investigation in Boise and Denver were hurrying to Cokeville to help negotiate the ransom. To be more accurate, they were hoping to talk the Youngs out of their extortion threats. When the bomb exploded, that wasn't necessary anymore. But they were still involved because it is a federal crime to kidnap or attempt to kidnap anyone. The agents from the Federal Bureau of Alcohol, Tobacco, and Firearms were also en route, pulled in by David Young's weapons violations.

In the matter of weapons, investigators turned up three guns the hostages didn't know the Youngs had. One of them was a .22 caliber pistol Doris carried in her purse. Another was the .22 caliber pistol David had tucked in the back of his trousers. In all, that made four guns on his person. Still another firearm the hostages didn't see was the .44 caliber "Bulldog" pistol found in the restroom with Young's body.

In some news accounts, a .44 Magnum was mentioned as one of the weapons used at the school by Young. If so, he returned it to the hallway. Law officers found it there later alongside an AR-15 semi-automatic, a shotgun, and thirty blasting caps (identified as "bombs" in some media coverage). Some of the confiscated rifles carried scopes, normally used for long-range outdoor shooting. Why did David bring them? Were they an indication he intended to leave with live hostages, and the scopes were for sighting on lawmen he expected to pursue him? Or did he want to take them on his journey into the Brave New World too? There were no answers. The scopes were simply another anomaly turned up by the investigation, as were the additional bomb wires and more guns than the Youngs could have used.

Lawmen found stores of gunpowder and ammunition and expected to find more guns in the Youngs' Tucson mobile home. They feared booby traps, according to the Pima County Sheriff's Office, but fortunately found none. Other bomb components and weapons were found in the Montpelier motel where the Youngs stayed before the takeover. In Tucson, they also found a note from Doris to Princess, inviting her to take whatever of Doris's jewelry she wanted. "To remember me by," the note concluded.

One of the central issues needing to be resolved for legal determinations—required before the case could be closed—was the question of how David and Doris died. The answer seemed obvious, but it had to be established officially and precisely. Even to confirm what was already assumed, painstaking investigative procedures had to be followed. Members of the ATF force helped in this determination. Wearing their navy blue coats with the large yellow ATF stenciled on the back, they were definitely a part of the scene. The investigation concluded that David had shot his wife after she caught fire from the explosion.

Carroll said that David used the .44 Bulldog to shoot Doris. He fired two slugs, one of which missed her; the other killed her. One of the slugs, presumably the one that missed her entirely, was found in the ceiling tile. The other slug remained in her body. Lawmen concluded that David must have been shooting upward from a low angle in the smoke-filled room.

Some of the investigators were displeased that Doris's body had been removed from the blood-spotted southwest corner of the room where she apparently died. Moving a body from its crime scene always negatively impacts an investigation—evidence can too easily be shifted, destroyed, or otherwise compromised. The EMTs explained, however, that they thought they were removing an adult hostage who might respond to mouth-to-mouth resuscitation. It was an understandable judgment call made in the midst of physical danger without the luxury of time to ponder all possible consequences.

Just after shooting Miller, but before killing Doris, Young had come face to face with Eva Clark and her children running past the bathroom door, yet he did not shoot them. This remained one of the many unanswered questions of the entire ordeal.

Another mystery is why he chose to return to the bathroom after shooting his wife instead of killing himself right after shooting her. Evidence showed he placed his .44 caliber beneath his chin and pulled the trigger. His body was not found till much later, slumped in a corner near a child-size toilet. Officers say the weapon used was apparently his favorite: a custom-made pistol bearing the serial number DGY-1 (David Gary Young, Number One).

One of the facts to be determined before the body was turned over to relatives was whether Young had indeed committed suicide. According to the angle of the cartridge entry and the powder burns caused by firing at a close range, suspicions were confirmed and the body was removed.

Local teens were recruited to search the school grounds "inch by inch" to mark "anything which appeared to be out of kilter" with what was there before the Youngs arrived. Some of the items could well have been left by kids during recess or lunch hour, or have fallen from pockets of firemen and EMTs running toward the smoldering classroom. Everything was flagged with a pink marker on a wire stick, hundreds piercing the grounds like so many pins in a giant pin cushion.

One of the most frustrating aspects of the investigation was the attempt to determine exactly why David left the classroom for the restroom. His autopsy confirmed that the reason did not have to do with his diabetic condition; he did not have his insulin supplies on his person when he left for the bathroom, and none were found in the room itself. No other signs of diabetic distress were evident, and yet several witnesses noted he was sweating profusely. What, if anything, that had to do with his leaving the room is not known.

All the other hypotheses focused on his state of mind, and there could be no exact determination of that, yet something caused him to become tense and anxious as the afternoon wore on. Apparently, it continued to mount until it became more than he could handle. Though he had hinted that he was prepared to hold everyone hostage for as long as ten days, he buckled under some kind of pressure in less than three hours.

The perplexing question raises an even more fundamental one about the nature of David Young himself. This was a man who was known for his methodical rejection of emotionalism, a man whose life was, if the diaries are to be believed, focused on making practical plans for an eternal existence that would bridge what he saw as the abyss between this life and the next. This would leave him successful and triumphant over the whining of common people who couldn't understand him and the obstructions of officials who were only standing in his way. He certainly saw himself as a disciplined and superior thinker who left nothing to chance. Yet the evidence shows that his plan to take the Cokeville Elementary School hostage was filled with inconsistencies and seeming errors of judgment.

For instance, he told the children they were not to use the water fountain or the restroom—over a ten-day period of time? Or did he already know that the takeover period would be far shorter than the time span he implied to his victims?

Why did David, with a reputation for being so meticulous, wait so long to obtain the gasoline container? Whether he found his jug at the Cokeville dump or brought one with him from elsewhere, how could he fail to check for a possible leak? And why did he choose such a complicated explosive device, requiring substantial labor to wire together correctly? It was certainly a visible threat to the hostages and helped keep them cowed and obedient; it was also bulky and dangerous to drag around.

Why did he react as he did to Princess's outburst, letting her leave with his only means of escape? Surely he realized she would be free to contact authorities, almost before he could effectively secure the building.

Why did he meticulously focus his plan around "highly intelligent" children to people his "Brave New World," but include teachers, for whom he had only disdain, among his hostages? Did he presume to be the one who would "reincarnate" a select few of his own choosing?

Why did he disdain human companionship and normal social interaction for the most part, and yet gather around him—for the perpetration of his one great masterstroke—a set of colleagues that included a cousin, a business investor, and a former coworker, as well as his wife and daughter? The "fun and games" reference made in his diary just prior to the takeover seems almost ludicrously at odds with his much more frequent and well-documented preference for self-isolation.

Finally, why did a man who apparently so carefully oversaw every facet of the hostage takeover, abruptly leave it all to his wife and disappear into the restroom? None of the hostages report his giving Doris any instructions before he changed the trigger string from his wrist to hers. He just did so and left.

Some witnesses observed that just before David turned the bomb over to Doris and headed to the restroom, he was sweating profusely. If his physical illness did not cause him to leave the classroom, what did? There could be no exact determination of his state of mind (only reasonably logical speculation), and hostages became convinced that something specifically caused David to become tense and anxious as the afternoon wore on. They felt this something mount until it became more than David could handle.

Some of the children said they felt something strange happening in the room. One described a brighter light, "orange-y or golden," while others thought it was a presence. One of the women held captive said she felt "sure we were going to die . . . and then shortly after realized I was planning what to fix for dinner!" Could this change in mood have been a reason why David Young sought refuge, even if temporarily, in the restroom?

Perhaps one key to solving this puzzle is the knowledge that David consistently acted for his own best interests, regardless of the outcome for others. A relative, speaking about David's refusal to end his exploitation of his daughters, said of the dead kidnapper, "He just did anything he wanted and thought he could get away with it. Too often, he did!"

The diaries reveal that David simply didn't perceive the will or choice of anyone else to be as valid as his own. Investigator Ron Hartley determined, after months of intense scrutiny of the writings, that he not only didn't but also couldn't consider other people's needs and feelings. Life and death had lost the shapes and relationships they have for most people on the planet.

Earl Carroll reiterated what other investigators had said about Young's intentions. "It doesn't appear from all the evidence that David Young ever planned on walking from the school building alive."

By an early age, his intellect and ego were little tempered by any overt compassion for others. With few social contacts, there was not much opportunity to determine how far out of line he might have been with the rest of the world. He was dangerous because of a fanatical compulsion to prove that he was always right. Young's mind seems to have taken him into more than a mere wrestling match with logic. Life may have become more and more bitter, as he faced the ugly realization that his profound conclusions had not brought him any meaningful satisfaction. After all his years of pondering, where indeed was his reward?

Chapter Eight

Love Pours In

"Our freedom was intact, our children were alive. Pain would pass, burns would heal. God does hear and answer prayers."
—Sherrie Cornia, mother of three hostages

While David Young's attack was against the children, he had targeted the whole community, and the fact that everyone survived was worth celebrating. The townspeople of Cokeville had every reason to feel jubilant. Even though the crisis had lasted less than three hours, every hostage was in grave jeopardy while it lasted. Five minutes of genuine danger can be frightening enough. Three hours must have seemed an eternity of fear and frustration to the captives inside, who were helpless to break free, and to their families outside who were helpless to aid them.

Had most or all of the hostages died, it is not impossible to imagine the town dying with them. It would have been too painful to stay in a place that only reminded survivors of how much they had lost. Townsfolk exulted, therefore, when they fully understood how marvelous the escape from the school had been: 150-odd children and adults trapped in a single room as a bomb designed for maximum destruction went off inside it. By surviving their ordeal, the victims of David Young had turned their town into a symbol of something extraordinarily powerful; not the explosive force of the bomb itself but the transcending force of the love that unified the hostages and gave them the courage and wit to outlast their attackers.

Sharing the wonder and jubilation felt by the community, people from surrounding towns and from all over the world poured out their feelings in letters, cards, posters, banners, phone calls, and personal visits.

The support shown the hostages came in a flood of incredible intensity. Extended family members kept Cokeville's phone lines hot with messages of hope and concern. Encouragement came from old friends, stunned by news that struck so close to home. People from all over felt compassion and empathy and took the time to express it.

One letter included a warm and sensitive poem about courage and a reminder that "what we make of ourselves with the time given in this life is what matters most." The letter was permeated with love. Its author was a youngster dying of leukemia.

Numerous letters included money, donated to help alleviate the mounting medical costs of those injured in the flames. A fund was set up for "The Cokeville Kids." From coast to coast, messages and donations swamped the little post office—over $16,000 was collected in the first few days. The money that flowed in was enough to cover hospital and doctor expenses for every child injured. These gifts from well-wishing strangers were especially appreciated, because some of the most serious injuries involved children from families who were out of work or struggling.

A Lutheran minister sent heartfelt wishes from his congregation: "We will be praying for all of you in church Sunday. God bless, as you now attempt to recover and to put yesterday in the past. Have a good day and a better tomorrow."

The pastor of St. Margaret Mary Church in Algonquin, Illinois, shared a poignant message from his parishioners: "Our parish community has witnessed the power of prayer . . . part of our parish were members of the pilgrimage group hijacked on TWA's flight 847 last June. Therefore, we are very understanding of what you have just gone through."

Some months after the bombing, a fifteen-foot-long banner arrived from a Latter-day Saint Primary in Bakersfield, California. Covered with hearts and the words "Our hearts reach out to you," it bore photos of dozens of children aged three to twelve. Messages with the photos indeed warmed the hearts of their readers: "I'm nine years old. I am glad you are safe." From other nine-year-olds: "Glad you are all rite," and "My name is Mike. I am glad you guys didn't die." An eleven-year-old drew a hand-held bomb: "I hope you are OK. You are lucky the bomb didn't work. P.S. Come to Bakersfield. You'll like it." Another invitation was even more compelling: "Please come to Bakersfield and see my skateboard." Teachers of the organization wrote, "Our Primary loves you all! Best wishes to you!"

A man in California, who preferred to remain anonymous, sent each of the worst burn victims a Cabbage Patch doll, not purchased from the store, but donated from his own private, highly treasured collection. He said he wanted to help the Cokeville kids cope. Such expressions as these without doubt helped the victims heal. They saw tangible evidence pour in which proved that, even if there were demented strangers out there who might bring them harm, there were also many, many more caring, genuinely concerned and loving strangers who would sacrifice personal time and means to bring them joy. This outpouring of love set the town on the first steps to recovery.

Before the hostages and their families could put the anger of the takeover behind them, however, they would have to go through a period of difficult coping. Everyone was pretty much in agreement by now that something extremely unusual—something that had all the characteristics of genuine divine intervention—had taken place. That protection had accomplished its task and was now, perhaps, withdrawn. Responsibility for coming all the way out from under the shadow of David Young was now in the hands of the victims and townsfolk themselves.

Effects of the ordeal didn't take long to manifest themselves. Psychologists familiar with hostage trauma know that, as bad as physical injuries can be, the accompanying emotional injuries can be much more destructive and long lasting. While similar in many respects, there would also be some important differences between the emotional trauma that the victims suffered and the trauma their friends and families went through, waiting for the crisis to end.

In our own home, we began to deal with the aftermath of the psychological damage—and we began to work on healing. Kam, huddled in a quilt in our living room, had just answered extensive questions from reporters, including some from Salt Lake City's *Deseret News*. The reporters wrote, "In a trailer home about 6½ miles from Cokeville, Wyoming, Kamron Wixom sits on a couch, cross-legged, with a patchwork quilt draped around his shoulders. He just finished talking long distance to a reporter from New York—not an everyday experience for the 12 year-old sixth grader. But neither is a bombing of a school room a common experience in this sleepy town of 550 people."

"I felt kinda mad. Now I feel shaky," Kamron told the reporters.

"Will you be scared to return to school next week?" reporters asked Kam.

"Not really," he said, "'cause I know they're both dead."

But by now, it became apparent to family members that Kamron was beginning to feel the "shakiness" he had earlier mentioned.

We began the difficult process of making sure our family members knew all was well. Our oldest daughter, Wendi, had not seen her brother Kamron in two years. Unable to reach us by telephone due to jammed phone lines, she waited hours for any word. That evening, a neighbor boy brought a newspaper to her home.

"Is this your mom and little brother?" he asked Wendi, knowing she was from Cokeville. Wendi grabbed the boy and the newspaper in one big, excited swoop and gave both of them a hug.

She recognized the jacket her mother was wearing. "It was your camp jacket," she explained later. "I looked at that picture and thought how that jacket would smell of campfire, and all the fun times we've had on our outings came flooding back. The photo came alive to me," she said, "and helped me feel a part of the family circle. I needed to be in contact with my family during this crisis."

That night, her newspaper ran the same photo again with the headline, "Photo eases worry for Safford woman."

"It was the first time I could visualize that my family was fine," she told the paper.

In the meantime, hearing reports on our car radio about "a bomb exploding in a school classroom in Cokeville, Wyoming," we worried about what other friends and relatives might think. It would be very easy to imagine the worst.

Judene's mother, Gladys, was somewhere in New York on vacation, and our daughter Julie was in Virginia. Two other children, Peggy and Wade, were working for the season as guides on the Colorado River, away from telephones for a week or more. They needed to be informed. Getting through to them seemed impossible. Phone calls were now coming in from other family members. One sister reported what she had seen on television. "Bomb kills two, injures 75 in Cokeville, Wyoming elementary school explosion . . . details later." Another sister, Julie, with extensive medical training in the Navy, heard reporters say something about the hostages having "black on their bodies like hot oil." She was horrified. "I knew the painful and destructive power of such a thing," she said, and she was gratified to learn the full story, which did not include anything about "hot oil."

We learned later that Judene's mother had been watching television at the home of friends in Poughkeepsie, New York. Someone called her attention to the Cokeville story, and she watched incredulously for more details. "I couldn't quite grasp the reality of it all," she later said. She tried unsuccessfully for two hours to call. It wasn't until the morning newspaper the next day had that photo of daughter and grandson embracing that she was reassured her family members were safe.

A Cokeville native, Barbara Perry, was driving through Donner Pass with her husband and caught news of what had happened in her hometown. The broadcast out of California said two people in Cokeville had been killed after teachers and children were taken hostage. Her husband described her as "frantic." She had relatives who were teachers and feared they might be the two who were dead. It was thirty-six hours before they were finally able to hear the whole story.

Every story added impact of what was unfolding before us. How far-reaching would it be? It brought to mind something Doris Young had told the children. "Think of this as an adventure—something to tell your grandchildren about." It was not quite what Mrs. Young had in mind, but if adventure can be defined as "a hazardous risk or remarkable experience," at least she was right about that part before she died.

Many families would deal with the trauma in different ways. Some would take the same attitude they did when the January temperature dipped to 50°F below, or when they were kicked by a cow: "When the going gets tough, the tough get going." But there was something different here, not only because it struck close to home, but also because it was more than physical adversity. There was much emotional sorting out to do. Not just for the hostages' personal feelings about themselves, but for others too.

None of the hostage children had ever encountered so many new challenges in a single afternoon. This was not like something they could turn off like TV. The matter focused on the youngster's faith in himself and mankind. Trust and ability to love responsibly was, in essence, the future ladder to inner-personal growth.

How would parents respond to help their children? Tougher, or more lenient? With discipline? Just love? It would be a learning experience for everyone.

Several parents with children who had been held hostage quickly saw that trying to force the memory away didn't solve their children's problems. Here was a matter to be more than reacted to—it had to be understood. For example, a child writing "crazy" and "insane" over a photograph of David Young's face might be a prosecuting attorney's nightmare, but it seemed excellent therapy to parents. When Kamron did just that, the entire family understood the full meaning behind the picture with the scribbled words on it.

Just before bedtime was not a good time for former hostages to be watching television. Terror, hostages, bombs, buildings exploding, guns in Iran or Nicaragua or elsewhere, brought former horror back to mind. Even some teachers held hostage had to leave lights on at night.

Teacher Janel Dayton said, "During the actual crisis, we had to be careful not to sympathize too much, or the children would take a clue from us that it was worse than they thought it was; but we gave a measure of sympathy, yes."

***

The most common problem faced by hostage victims is an overwhelming sense of fear and vulnerability. Tina Cook, first to be confronted by David Young and first to be taken hostage, found returning to her school duties difficult. One day a man stepped up to the receptionist's desk and seemed to be stalling. She panicked. Finally, he asked for Mr. Excell—he was just there to check out the playground equipment.

On another day, while Tina was speaking with a visitor, the woman fished around in her purse. Tina immediately imagined a gun. When the woman found what she wanted, it was a business card; she was a sales representative on call. In addition to incidents like these, Tina had recurring nightmares of David Young walking up and thumping on the counter. "Here I am, Mrs. Cook," he would say, "and you didn't think I'd come back, did you?" It took her months to get the man's arrogant superiority and the fear she felt that day out of her mind.

One of the custodians for the school, whose child had been a hostage, told Principal Excell she could not work in the building anymore after dark. The principal himself said it gave him "an eerie feeling" to turn a key in the school door when he came there alone several days after the takeover "with the memories so fresh in [his] mind."

Memorial Day, ten days after the incident, resulted in nervous moments for some of the hostage boys but at the same time allowed them to move past their fears. The local Boy Scouts were asked to assist the American Legion post in commemorating the community dead. The boys felt very lucky not to be among those honored that year. At the appropriate moment in the ceremonies came a twenty-one-gun salute. It sounded "a little too close" to the young assistants. "I jumped when the guns blew off near me," one boy said. "But we made it. I think we're going to be OK."

One kindergartner would have a much harder time recovering. Her personality changed after the takeover—not even her own family members could find the old enthusiasm in her. "The burns had healed. The rest hadn't," her mother said. Outgoing no longer, the little girl shut herself into a shell, hiding anytime she saw a man with a beard. When her father talked to a bearded man at their front door one day, she ran for a back bedroom. Hearing a firecracker at a family party, she disappeared and couldn't be found. After a long search, family members found her cowering in the barn.

Townspeople were counseled that every person would move at his own pace and that traumatic events had anniversaries: "A year from now, for example, people will probably show increased anxiety."

Along with fear and anxiety, anger is recognized as an equally prevalent and genuine response to being victimized. At a town meeting held the Monday after the takeover, one citizen who had not been a hostage tried to apply some Christian charity by saying that perhaps the hostage-takers "didn't really want to hurt you."

The response was immediate, almost harsh: "How can anyone say they didn't mean to hurt us? They hauled all that crap in to kill people!"

A five-year-old had watched his father carry the body of a woman from the smoking classroom, taking "good care" of her. Then the boy realized the woman was the one who had tried to kill them. What did that say about his father? Another child named his emotion: he was "awfully, awfully mad."

In addition, there were the memories of terror and revulsion. Some children had crawled across a body and had attempted to help her, only to discover it was the woman who had threatened them. Such memories are not easily forgotten.

Problems would show up for months, even years—lives of the hostage families were not yet their own. Fathers and mothers, in search of security, found themselves putting down tougher rules. Mothers would jump at the falling of a pencil; fathers would berate them for being so touchy. Mothers got after fathers for being insensitive. Even weeks after the crisis, a mother said she cried at nothing. Confessed another, "I snap at every little thing." Such behavior, even when recognized, left the victims feeling guilty, further lowering their self-esteem.

Emotional trauma was especially hard to overcome when it involved a loss of trust. Teachers who had been taken captive struggled with this as much as the children did. Janel Dayton reported that yearbook photographers had nearly given her a heart attack by taking an impromptu flash picture of her working in her room. One day the grandmother of one of her students arrived unannounced to fetch her grandchild. "I'd never seen her before," Janel Dayton said. "She could have done that in the past and it wouldn't have mattered, but things were different now."

The younger children had special problems to overcome. Those aged six and seven were just beginning to build a sense of confidence and order in their lives. Now both were, if not shattered, at least shaken. Trust, in particular, was damaged. Love and obedience were now suspect. "We did what the adults told us to do, and we got hurt," was expressed by some. "What did we do wrong?" Many of the children began to feel guilty; they were taken hostage because, in some unknown way, they hadn't "measured up."

Children who had been some of Jean Mitchell's best huggers began to hold back. They were now aloof, sharing less love. She sorely missed their expressions of simple love. Yet she knew those emotions couldn't be forced. Jean felt the kids might be feeling betrayed by the world of grown-ups that had let this thing happen to them. She was fearful about the youngsters losing trust in her. They had obeyed her, with this result. She was not sure what she could say to them.

The slow process of working through fears and hostilities generated by the crisis went on among those who had not been taken hostage as well. Fear that precipitated a sense of vulnerability often manifested itself as parental over-protectiveness. Time and time again, mothers and fathers faced the mental hurdle of never wanting to let their young children out of sight, of not wanting to let them go back to school. Something as simple and familiar as a sonic boom could raise waves of panic and an intense desire to drop everything else and run to the child.

The anger felt by victims mirrored the anger felt by their families. One did not have to be present in the classroom to feel the trauma there, counselors explained. "Families and people who were outside of the town when things were happening will still have some very real and important feelings that need to be worked through."

Sam Bennion had reason to be angry. His wife, Pat, was substituting for Briant Teichert, away at the track meet, when the takeover occurred. She had to be hospitalized and suffered complications from the infections in her arms. His widowed mother, Verlene, was in school as teacher's aide and was injured while helping children escape through the windows. All three of the Bennion kids were among the hostages. Realistically, Sam had been threatened with the loss of his entire family. The anger and fear generated by that threat would not easily pass.

Delayed complications were often exhibited by parents rather than hostages. A number of adults were traumatized almost as much by what their mature imaginations told them could have happened as they were by what actually did. Thinking about the awful possibilities became a coping mechanism of its own, as the mind tried to admit the existence of unthinkable scenarios in order to face them down.

Understandably, some who entirely escaped the crisis had to struggle with feeling left out—unworthy of the test. The six children absent that day had missed the most important, dramatic thing ever to happen to their community. Morning kindergartners, eluding capture by half a day, felt the same—no one was paying attention to them. Had they also "not measured up" somehow?

The name given to reactions like these, which seem so inconsistent on the surface, is "survivor guilt." Most often seen in those who live when their fellow-hostages die in a violent confrontation, survivor guilt also hits those who are simply not involved while their friends or loved ones are suffering. No one in Cokeville envied those who had been burned in the aftermath of the explosion. Yet they wanted to know firsthand what had happened; they wanted to share the burden. Briant Teichert's absence from school the day of the takeover was particularly hard on him. The thought, he said, of substitute teacher Pat Bennion being harmed while taking his place "was just unbearable."

Older students, who felt guilty about not helping rescue their younger brothers and sisters, were themselves helped toward a more balanced frame of mind by the attending psychologists and counselors. "What if you had gone back," they were asked, "into the burning room? Wouldn't you just be in the way of people trying to get out quickly?" As the students answered such questions, they were able to realize that it was, indeed, unselfish to care so much about the other pupils, but that they did the right thing in getting quickly out of the way.

Families had to deal with the mundane responsibilities of daily life while they were also dealing with the serious emotional and physical burdens that the crisis forced upon them. One father, whose daughter was being treated for burns, later had a car wreck and had to be hospitalized himself—about the same time that his wife went to the hospital to give birth to unexpected twins. Fortunately for everyone, the showering of outside love and aid meant that no family had to lose their home or go hungry because they happened to cross the path of a confused and self-destructive man.

Occasionally, denial was seen as a practical way out of the crisis: "Let's not make too much of this whole thing. The kids are lucky to be alive. Let's forget about it and get on with our lives. The sooner we do it, the sooner the kids can do it." While the attitude was healthy in its effort not to wallow or dwell on the traumatic memories of their captive hours, most hostages and their parents realized that negative emotions were rising to the surface naturally and continually, and that it would be necessary to work through them, rather than deny them, before real healing could occur.

But the process could begin immediately. From the moment the children escaped and commenced the process of confronting what they had just experienced, parents and school officials in the town and psychologists who came from outside began a process of their own—offering the hostages positive ways of handling their physical and emotional upheaval.

Early on, townspeople were commended for immediately providing two positive experiences for the hostages. The first was total reassurance and the second was proper praise. When parents and other citizens were on hand to scoop up the first screaming youngster that crossed their paths, cuddling them personally or staying close while their parents were located, they provided crucial contrast to the detached, depersonalized malevolence David Young had shown. Familiar faces, familiar surroundings, behavior the children recognized as consistent and normal, even the sounds and smells they were used to helped them accept that they had really escaped from Room 4. However, while they would frequently relive the fear of their hours with David Young, they would also be able to relive the memory of people who welcomed them unconditionally back to normal life.

Lincoln County attorney Richard Leonard noted with amazement how well the local people were coping, even just after the takeover. "Here were people, in terror of their lives just two hours before," he said, "now serving drinks and sandwiches to out-of-town officials. They were bouncing back awfully fast, considering the circumstances. It was gratifying to see them recovering so quickly."

At the town meeting held the Monday after the crisis, everyone gathered to more formally assess what had happened. Dr. Allen Lowe, the district school superintendent, assured the listeners, "You have the prayers and support of many. There were many heroes to come out of the tragedy last Friday, including you and your children. Our purpose is to rebuild, restore, and strengthen."

At one point, teachers were singled out for their heroic efforts, particularly those who kept themselves and the children calm in the face of danger. The audience rose to applaud them. The children themselves were praised for obeying teachers and summoning up a brave front for each other. Peace officers from other areas, who had come in to assist Cokeville's lawmen, praised the entire town for its discipline. "You were a great example," one of them said.

Someone stood to commend the EMTs for their work; then another spoke in praise of the law enforcement officers. Everyone was thanking everyone. "In the eyes of professionals around the country who have handled very serious situations, you are to be commended," said Dr. Nohl Sandahl, head of the team of psychologists. "They stand in respect for how you have come out of this situation. You did things right." Teachers wanted to convince the children that they had experienced a severe trial and passed it with flying colors. Parents and other adults were counseled to show confidence; children can handle what parents can handle, townspeople were reminded.

Talking and listening, as the townspeople did at this meeting, was the next critical step in healing. Shock was wearing off. People needed to tell each other where they were when the bomb went off. Never had so much happened in such a short time in the town. Never had so many intense and diverse emotions been generated.

Rocky Moore took what he called a "realistic" attitude. "I wish David Young was here right now. Take away his guns and I'd like to have my hands on him—right now."

"Do you hate him?" Rocky was asked.

"You bet I do. I love hating him." At least Rocky could talk in a positive way about the negative feelings he felt for the man who held him and the others hostage.

Dr. Sandahl and his team of psychologists were barraged with questions. "My child won't talk about it, yet it seems that he hurts inside. If we ask why, he changes the subject. What should we do?"

"Be supportive and open," they were told. "Let them know they can talk about it freely when they're ready."

"Some of the things I'm hearing from my child are gross and aggressive," said a parent.

"Just listen," was the reply. "Some language or behavior may seem inappropriate for a while. Don't let it shock or disturb you, but broaden your tolerance level to help them work through their feelings."

The children wanted to know if the Youngs were "bad people." They were told, "Like machinery, people can sometimes go awry. These people did bad things."

Said one mother, "My child saw his father pull a rifle out from the truck today and was terrified."

The psychologists knew the reaction well: "Such reminders will initiate fear. This hunting community will have a lot of that."

Another mother said, "My son doesn't really know what happened. When people talk about it, he isn't sure he knows what happened, and he was there."

Said another, "My daughter says she will never go in Room 4 again."

Counselors from around the country came, wrote, or called in to urge the parents just to listen to their children. "Don't even think of what you are going to say next. Simply listen, even if you say nothing." Listening became as natural as breathing. As neighbor listened to neighbor, parent to child, classmate to classmate, love poured in.

School district officials suggested that teachers begin working with therapists the following Tuesday to learn how they could best help the students start school again. It would be vital for teachers to talk through their own problems before helping the kids with theirs. It was decided that counseling would be made available on a walk-in basis and for as long as necessary. "We hesitate to put a time limit on it," officials explained, as each victim works through his fears independently. Counseling would be available, furthermore, to anyone in town. "It is important that no feelings in the community be held in," the psychologists stressed.

Guidelines were taken from a program called Project Cope, provided by the Community Services of the San Diego California Mental Health Department. Five- to eleven-year-olds should, the recommendations read, be offered a physical reenactment of the disaster to provide clarification of what had happened. That was one reason school officials made Room 4, still in the condition they had left it on Friday, available to the children and their parents the following Sunday.

The room was open all that day, and except for a tarp thrown on the floor in the room's southwest corner, where Doris's body was found, everything was left untouched. There was even a pair of shoes left behind. Children visiting the room were heard to ask if the owner had been blown right out of them.

Tentatively at first, children with their parents relived the scene inside the blackened room. "This is where I sat," said one.

"I was coloring right here at this desk," pointed out another.

The children were putting the pieces together in their minds. Some noticed a message scrawled in black on the wall. "Help," it read. Others took time to write their names in the soot. Nearly all the children had asked if they had to return to the hostage site. When they were told no, they went anyway. They didn't want to be there, yet, as one child said, "I had to."

"Reestablishment of ownership is an important part of the healing process," school psychologists told parents and teachers.

Older children were encouraged, said the guidelines, to talk about the disaster and share their feelings, to rehearse safety measures to be taken in the future, and to express any deep feelings of loss or grieving. School officials told the parents that, as the guidelines predicted, "performance levels in various academic and other skills might drop off for a time—but parents and teachers should reassure the youngsters [that] competency will return."

One important question was when school would resume. Summer vacation was just around the corner. District officials felt that no matter how little work was accomplished in the final days, it was important for the children not to wait three months before returning. At the same time, psychologists felt it necessary to ease students back into school sessions. Students were invited to return when they felt up to it. Most came for a few hours on Wednesday, the first day classes were resumed, then half a day Thursday, and all day Friday, a mere week after the takeover.

On that Wednesday, a few students returned with parents, but most came without them. "More than I expected," said school district counselor Mike Cummings. Cummings and local psychologist George Chournos spent the morning watching children arrive, looking for signs of any problems. "I saw five kids walk up here by themselves real early, and I just about bawled," Chournos said. As one who grew up on a rugged western sheep ranch, Chournos said it struck him that "some of these kids really are tough." He thought the therapy of teachers and children seeing each other again, this time in safe and normal surroundings, "was just as good for the teachers as it was for the children."

Teachers practiced encouraging their students to express whatever was on their minds, he noted later. "Where were you when the bomb went off?" Kliss Sparks asked her fourth graders.

Rusty Birch said he was right next to the lady on fire. "It took me about three seconds to figure out what was going on," he said. "Then I got out of there!"

A key approach to helping everyone leave behind the trauma and begin living normally again was the predictable one of seeking out activities that would reconstruct family and community ties. One such was a Little League Baseball game of alumni thirteen- to-fourteen-year-olds against the current nine- to-twelve-year-olds. Because the game was set for Saturday morning following the crisis, it was nearly canceled. Parents didn't think the kids would be up to it. But the kids voted yes, and the game was played.

There was an unusual twist to this event. Some of the children had baseball mitts and shoes in the school. Since it was less than a day after the takeover, the police cordon was still in place, sealing off the building. Even though bomb experts had combed the premises for any explosives, detonating them and removing all the weapons to be placed in evidence, investigators were still sifting the entire school property for additional clues needed in any future hearings.

The children were not to go inside. But hearing that they would need to enter only the north wing, which was nowhere near Room 4, a sympathetic sheriff's deputy listened to their requests. Still, permission was not given.

"Come on, don't you think we've suffered enough?" said one of the boys.

The compassionate deputy gave in. "Go get your mitts," he said.

On the following Wednesday, an event of particular importance was held—the annual high school spring concert, led by John Miller. There had been speculation that the concert would be canceled because Miller had been injured. His recovery was considered amazingly swift, but everyone wondered if he would be up to conducting an hour-long concert less than a week after being shot near the heart.

"I'm not in pain; I'm glad to be here," he announced to the packed auditorium. It was a simple statement, but it electrified the crowd. They erupted in a spontaneous standing ovation for Miller, for the children, for the teachers. It was also for the entire community. The applause lasted and lasted. People felt they were getting control of their lives again. It felt good to cheer, to whistle, to applaud.

John Miller was known as a quiet, private person who didn't often say much, except through his music. But on this night he wanted to share. A bit hesitant about embarrassing his wife, he proceeded to tell his friends and neighbors how hospital attendants had taken all his clothes in Montpelier and left him with little more than the traditionally awful, not-so-private hospital gown. In that garb he was airlifted to Bannock Memorial Hospital in Pocatello. When the nurse came in to record the valuables that arrived with him, she started at the top and began ticking off the long list of possibilities. John could see it was a very extensive list. "I told her I could save her some time," he said to the crowd. "I have nothing with me but my shorts!"

The audience roared with laughter. When they had quieted a bit, he added wryly, "Thank goodness for those shorts."

John also shared that when he was waiting to be taken to the examining room, he was visited by his Episcopal minister, Reverend Lawrence Perry, and the Reverend Gerald Sullivan of Cokeville's Catholic parish. "We would like to give you a blessing," they said.

"I would very much like you to give me a blessing," he replied.

"You might say," said Father Sullivan, "that we're the SWAT team for God."

The audience's applause transcended religious boundaries. The room was full of sheer joy. "The healing process is well underway if we can laugh like this," Sherrie Cornia said to the people seated nearby.

The next Friday, Ford Brothers Circus came to town, and Principal Excell, the Mitchells, Rocky Moore, and others raced the elephants down Main Street. "Oh, it felt good," a teacher said. "For a time I forgot all about everything." Delighted youngsters cheered for their favorite teacher. At the circus, it was noted that some rides were shunned because the attendants had beards. Mostly, however, it was a particularly happy time.

"It was fun," said one boy. "I ate everything I ever wanted!"

A case of overindulgence? One father understood the importance of an unfettered good time. "I was happy to give them the opportunity for one night."

Another remarkably positive activity was provided by one of the Salt Lake City television stations, KUTV. In conjunction with Lagoon, an amusement park north of Salt Lake City, they put together a special party for all the hostages. It lasted a full summer day, and the station spent thousands of dollars to bus hostages and their families to the amusement park, providing lunch as well. The children soaked up this kind of love—translated into something they could get their hands on. The bumper cars, merry-go-rounds, hot dogs, and punch were all additional salve to the wounds received on that bizarre day in mid-May.

Positive activities needed to be accompanied by positive mental attitudes. Some of the adults set the example by saying that they would simply wait out the day when the pain would go away. "Every good thing happens in due time," John Teichert said. Bibles were pulled out and hostages and family members read them together. Scripture reading, uplifting sayings from literature, writing, and reading poems—any source of optimism and strength was used as a road map to healing.

Cokeville clergymen counseled their church members to pray that they could purge their memories of hate over this ordeal. LDS bishop John Teichert pointed out how prayer had "helped from the beginning of this crisis."

At the hospitals, administrators and physicians, prepared for a wave of victims, found most children "highly cheerful" despite painful second and third degree burns. "By golly," said one physician, "their attitude appears to be helping their recovery. I was amazed at how quickly all of the burns I saw healed." Rod Jacobsen, administrator of the Bear Lake Memorial Hospital in Montpelier, said, "Everyone noticed right away" that the kids were not feeling sorry for themselves or harboring self-pity. "They just wanted to do what had to be done."

Nine days after the bomb exploded, Gina Taylor, who came near to losing her eye in the blast, participated in a church program where her father spoke. As she sang "I Am a Child of God," she was able to watch the audience with both eyes. The only evidence of her injuries was a little white patch on her face where she had been burned. "Lead me, guide me, walk beside me. Help me find the way," came the words. Perhaps they had never been felt as deeply.

In time, doctors said that only a few victims would carry permanent scars or have long months of slow recovery from extensive burns, like Billie Jo Hutchinson would. "That in itself is something of a miracle," said one parent, "judging from what the doctors first feared."

Many people did not want the unique aspects of their escape to be forgotten. Said one woman, "I think this should be remembered as a miracle of the same magnitude as the parting of the Red Sea."

One of the most memorable comments was made by Tina Cook: "Deep down I don't want to ever forget how bad this was because I don't want to ever forget how good it eventually turned out either."

The town itself took an action that further underscored its independence and ability to recover—it politely refused state aid. "The town is so self-sufficient," said Audrey Cotherman, of Wyoming's Department of Education, "that it has not needed state aid and has done very well on its own resources. Cokeville is the most remarkable community we've ever seen. Those people responded and organized themselves. I cannot praise the community enough."

In their efforts to heal themselves and their children and neighbors, the citizens had to move through one of the most difficult but important steps of recovery: forgiving themselves and others. As the town pulled tightly together, it seemed for a time that one person was virtually forgotten. She was the only person in the entire community who had lost a loved one—Bernie Petersen, Doris Young's daughter.

Not only had she lost her mother, but she was also afraid she had also lost her friends. At first, she was merely shocked. "My own mother doing something like that? I kept asking myself why she would endanger children's lives that way. Could I have stopped her? I felt guilty—but I had no idea. We loved living here in Cokeville," she explained. "My husband was born and raised here. This is his home." Despite their love for Cokeville, the Petersens did not want to stay in a place where they were resented for their familial connection to the terrorists.

Some people in town had to work through the animosity in their own minds. It was difficult for them to be reminded of the horror they experienced at the hands of David and Doris. Some neighbors just didn't know what to say to the Petersens. The first to find the words were the Morfelds, parents of one of the most seriously burned children, Tina. Bernie was assured they did not blame her for what happened. More encouraged, the Petersens wrestled with their feelings. Then they decided to stay.

Ralph Waldo Emerson said about prayer, "Prayer is a contemplation of the facts of life from the highest possible point of view" ("Transcendental Idealism," *The American Tradition in Literature* [WW Norton and Co.: New York, 1956], 350). Had the prayers of all these humble children on their knees toppled the kingdom of an arrogant philosopher on his tiptoes?

Part of the therapy for everyone included learning more details of the incident—how the hostages had won their trial by terror. With school and community psychologists offering services without cost to the parents or hostages, many took advantage of this opportunity to talk things over. It was a positive approach, meeting an obstacle and overcoming it.

We discovered that the full impact of the crisis was not felt by many families right at first. One woman said, "I had just naively thought that things would work out. When I realized later the entire story, I couldn't believe how nonchalant I had been."

Few who had been inside Room 4 wanted to talk of hating the perpetrators. They wanted to forget it. The best way to do that was to not talk much about it—for a time. Then, no one could keep it inside.

The process of gathering information for this book brought some painful moments. One afternoon while alone, looking over photographs, Judene felt overwhelmed upon seeing them. In some newspaper pictures, the devastation of the hostage classroom was shown clearly. She recalled the heavy smell of old smoke as she visited that room following the explosion. Then there was the close-up shot of David Young's shopping cart with little left of its twisted frame. Somehow, all the objectively gathered facts swept together in a whirlwind of emotion. She wrote in her diary, "My son! He was there in that room, only six feet away from that shopping cart. We came that close to losing him . . . to not having his loving arms and bright spirit in our lives. . . ."

"And then the sobs came. Great heaving sobs that almost left me gagging. I felt strangely out of control, as if emotion from some other source had taken over my body. Yet through it all, I was aware that the sobs were also of deep gratitude—an overwhelming gratitude that this thing had NOT been what it could have been. Then the crying stopped more suddenly even than it had begun."

That same scenario could be happening in many other families . . . and the healing would continue.

In one of the many ironies of the takeover, that which had lured David to town in the first place—its strong family ties—now began to mitigate and dissipate what he had planned. David had been defeated by the very love and unity that he believed was Cokeville's vulnerable point. He had manipulated that love to take control; now his victims were allowing it to come in and learning how to use it to walk free of his memory.

An editorial in the Salt Lake City *Deseret Morning News*, one week after the incident, contained this comment: "If a lesson emerges from this episode, it is a lesson about what can happen to individuals who start nursing a grievance, real or imagined—who convince themselves they are right and everyone else is wrong. . . . As was so graphically demonstrated by the Cokeville madness, people can poison themselves with their own ideas."

Life will not be taken for granted in Cokeville as casually as it was before. Its preciousness is too highly valued. There is more understanding and more compassion now. Had David Gary Young understood such emotions, he might never have done what he did.

Among the many letters from the nation was one from a retired elementary teacher in a rural South Dakota town. Her words aptly expressed the truths learned by the children and parents of Cokeville as they moved away from their ordeal and back toward real life: "Fear is a counterfeit of faith. When we put faith to work, it will always overcome fear. Love always overcomes hate. The counterfeit of anything is never as powerful as the real thing."

Afterword

Many testimonies of divine intervention were given to us as authors of this book that survivors did not want to be made public. After all, something like a spiritual manifestation comes with a feeling of what can only be described as sacred trust. Although some mentioned the word "miracle" to us as writers of this work, they did not want their names to be included. What the reader is getting here is, in some ways, the tip of an iceberg.

It is easy to imagine the hurt some survivors felt as they were growing up when classmates at school questioned or even taunted them. For that reason, some of the conversations we have had with survivors, including close friends, may not be included herein. As even some faculty members have reiterated with us, "We hope those who receive our testimonies will respect our privacy and refrain from raining us with calls for which we may not have time to address [each one]. . . . In addition, some survivors experienced such pain in David Young's takeover into the sanctuary of their school that day that they still do not want to talk about it. Not all were even happy to have further mention of such a painful ordeal. "

But as survivor Lori Nate Conger was quoted saying in the Deseret News of March 19, 2015, "I firmly believe this is a story that needs to be told."

Katie Walker said in the same article, "Our brains didn't process then because we were so young [age 7]. It's taken years to sort through this. It taught us at a very young age that the Lord answers our prayers and it helped create a pretty unique bond in our town. We were not alone."

First grade teacher Janel Dayton admitted, "I was one of the faculty members who just wanted to forget the entire ordeal we suffered through when Mr. Young overtook the school. With time, and further thought, however, I was among many who realized that something special happened that day. . . . We were truly blessed with help from above. I join many others in thanking the Lord for looking after all of us in the school, to thwart the evil plans which obviously failed. Now, I feel that we must give our gratitude for . . . all that we can call 'Divine Intervention.' We would be ungrateful if we did not pay tribute to this miracle."

Appendix I

Witness to Miracles

On May 16, 2006, the community of Cokeville, Wyoming, held a "Remembrance Day." On this special occasion, survivors and law enforcement officials gathered to share their personal accounts of what took place in Cokeville twenty years earlier. The overwhelming message of all in attendance was that they had experienced a miracle. "If you don't believe that this was [d]ivine intervention, then you were not there that day," said one law enforcement official. Many who shared this thought, including sheriffs deputies, highway patrolmen, town policemen, firemen, and medics were not members of any church.

Those who want to read the many detailed personal testimonies of what survivors and law enforcement officials termed divine intervention should read the book *Witness to Miracles*. The conviction that God blessed them in answer to their prayers that day in the Cokeville Elementary School was shared by dozens of survivors, students and faculty, in detailed testimonies compiled in the book *Witness to Miracles*. The book was published by the nonprofit organization, The Cokeville Miracle Foundation, Cokeville, Wyoming, 83114.

***

Several of the hostages consented to be interviewed, and their oral histories are part of a collection by Sue Castenada entitled *Survivor is My Name: Voices of the Cokeville Elementary School Bombing*. A compilation of these recordings can be accessed at http://www.wyohistory.org/

encyclopedia/cokeville-elementary-school-bombing.

Full recordings and transcripts of the individual interviews are available at the following site: http://www.wyohistory.org/oral-histories. Search the list for "Cokeville survivor oral history."

Carol Peterson, second grade teacher: http://www.wyohistory.org/oral-histories/second-grade-teacher-carol-petersen

Glenna Walker, mother of students: http://www.wyohistory.org/oral-histories/emt-glenna-walker-cokeville

Jamie Buckley King, third grade student at time of bombing: http://www.wyohistory.org/oral-histories/third-grade-student-jamie-buckley-king-cokeville

Janel Dayton, first grade teacher: http://www.wyohistory.org/oral-histories/first-grade-teacher-janel-dayton-cokeville

Kathy Davison, Emergency Management Coordinator, dispatcher: http://www.wyohistory.org/oral-histories/emergency-management-coordinator-kathy-davison-1986-bombing-cokeville-elementary-scho

Kevin Walker, fireman and parent: http://www.wyohistory.org/oral-histories/emergency-management-coordinator-kathy-davison-1986-bombing-cokeville-elementary-scho

Kliss Sparks, fourth grade teacher: http://www.wyohistory.org/oral-histories/fourth-grade-teacher-kliss-sparks

LeaKae Roberts Weston, fourth grade student at time of bombing: http://www.wyohistory.org/oral-histories/fourth-grade-student-leakae-roberts-weston

Rachel Walker Hollibaugh, third grade student at time of bombing: http://www.wyohistory.org/oral-histories/third-grade-student-rachel-walker-hollibaugh

Rich Haskell, certified bomb technician: http://www.wyohistory.org/oral-histories/certified-bomb-technician-rich-haskell-1986-bombing-cokeville-elementary-school

Ron Hartley, Lead Investigator, father of four student survivors: http://www.wyohistory.org/oral-histories/lead-investigator-ron-hartley

Tina Cook, school secretary: http://www.wyohistory.org/oral-histories/secretary-tina-cook

Appendix II

Kamron Wixom's Accounts

Kamron Wixom
Press Release

Press release written by Kamron Wixom to help answer questions of concerned family and friends.

The BOMB
By Kam Wixom

COKEVILLE (May 16, 1986)—Our sixth grade class was on a bathroom break when a lady came up to us and said, "Go in the first grade room, and we have a surprise for you." Our teacher, Mr. Mitchell, asked what kind of surprise. She said, "You'll find out."

The teachers told us the man in the room had bombs, and we thought it was an assembly, that he was an expert helping us get through a possible Libyan attack. He said he was the "most wanted man in the culture." That was about all he said. He talked privately with some of the teachers who went up to him, and we learned he and the woman were holding us hostage until they could get $2 million for each of us. There were about 150 students gathered in this one classroom.

The man had three pistols attached to his belt, and they had two .22 rifles and an M1 leaning against the wall by the door. They had a metal shopping cart full of batteries, and an old milk jug filled with gasoline, and we could see metal wires for the trigger, some batteries, and copper coil inside. There were four or five explosives found later elsewhere in the school.

The sixth grade and some of the younger kids around us agreed we should say a prayer. We were all sitting on the floor. We folded our arms and Allyson Cornia just started saying a prayer for us. She said she wanted everybody to be safe, that we would all survive. We felt we had done our part in asking the Lord to help us. Now it was up to us to cooperate and do all we could.

A lot of kids were crying softly. All of us were scared, but some didn't want to show it because we knew it wouldn't do us any good. I thought, "I just don't want to get in trouble and have the bomb go off." None of us ever thought about going out of the room even though we were near the door that had been propped open. We didn't want to do anything they didn't want us to do. We asked the teachers how long we would have to stay there. They said, "Maybe ten days, maybe just a couple more hours."

The teachers were trying to get our minds off it by letting us watch TV and read books, and play games like Legos. Brenda Hartley and I built a tank out of Legos, complete with guns. I said to Brenda, "OK, men, we're going to cross the 'death lines' and blow 'em up." The "death line" was the tape on the floor that Mr. Mitchell had placed around the bomb and the man sitting on the desk next to it. He had said, "OK kids, we are going to play a game. This is the magic square, and if you pass it you'll be out." No one tried to get near the square. Brenda had laughed when I said what I did about our tank. Then we got up and went to the table near the door where some magnets were that we could play with.

We had all been in the room together now since about one thirty. It was now a little before four. The man had called his wife to come and hold the trigger to the bomb, and he went into the bathroom, which is connected to the classroom. He had been in there about two minutes. We were all beginning to feel a little more relaxed, then BOOM! I looked up and saw the ball of fire and a cloud of black smoke. The fire stayed low, but the smoke spread quickly through the room. There were pieces of paper in flames floating around the room and falling in front of me. Everybody started yelling and running. I went out the door and ran north toward the main doors. I was the first one to go through those doors, and ran on toward Main Street saying softly to myself, "I'm alive!"

Our band teacher, Mr. Miller, had run out of the school through the south doors and was shot in the back by the man, who had come out of the restroom when the bomb went off. Mr. Miller collapsed at the corner on Main Street near where I was standing.

There were ambulances, crowds of people searching for brothers and sisters with tears in their eyes. It was like I had come back into civilization after being out in the wilds alone. Kids were being hosed off to cool their burns. I went into Steve Taylor's house to call home, but no one was there. I went back out onto the street, looking for someone to leave a message with that I was going to go down to city hall with some of the other kids and get out of the crowd. That's when I saw Dad with his arm raised, and Mom with her arms open. I ran to them. I was sure glad to see them. Mom and I hugged for a long time, then Dad caught up to us and we had a three-way hug. I cried. It felt good to cry. I had been too mad to cry before.

Kam's Recollections as an Adult, Almost Thirty Years After the Incident, March 2015

After lunch recess ended, we filed inside for our thirty minutes of quiet reading time. Mr. Mitchell interrupted the silent reading and asked us if we noticed a smell of gasoline. Many of us did. He wondered if Delbert Rentfro, the custodian, was up to something like getting the riding lawn mower ready or something. We had taken a bathroom break and were heading back to class when we were approached by a lady we didn't know. She asked us to follow her; she said she had a surprise waiting for us in Room 4. Mr. Mitchell was visibly and audibly puzzled. He wondered why he didn't know anything about this surprise, seeing that his own wife was the teacher in that room.

As we followed her toward the room, Mr. Mitchell turned to us, asking if any of us knew who this woman was. No one knew. The door opened and the room was darkened, with many of the overhead fluorescent lights turned off. As I looked at the younger children's faces, they were somber. I wondered what was going on. I saw modeling clay on their desks and I wondered if they were showing off their creations or something. Looking to my left, I noticed M16s and other rifles leaning against the bulletin board that flanked the chalkboard on the north wall of that room. I thought there must be some kind of gun safety assembly or something like that.

Mr. Moore waved Mr. Mitchell over to talk. I was right next to them as Mr. Moore said, "This man has a bomb and is holding us hostage." Mr. Mitchell and I turned and noticed the brooding, bearded man near the center of the room. The sound in Mr. Moore's voice told me he was serious, and his manner seemed very subdued, very not like the boisterous Irish-rooted mountain man we all knew and loved as the fifth grade teacher. Our class found places on the floor near the fifth graders. Hearing the words "hostage" and "bomb," my mind went straight to the current events that we had been talking about in class.

Far away, in Libya, a man named Muammar Gaddhafi was using terrorists to be a bully in the world, telling American military ships that if they crossed "the death line," as Gaddhafi had called it, that he would shoot and sink them. I had drawn pictures of these so-called "terrorists." I had depicted the terrorists as red ants in every one of them. Mr. Moore had printed out an image of Gaddhafi with targets encircling his face. I asked if I could use it for my dartboard at home. It became shredded over time.

I knew the man in our room was not Gaddhafi, but I wondered if he was part of something bigger. I immediately thought of the movie *Red Dawn* I'd seen. I imagined paratroopers landing on the grounds of schools all over the United States, just like in the movie. I looked out the window to the school grounds . . . but there was nothing like that.

My mind was trying to process all of it. I asked Mr. Mitchell if it was some sort of drill to prepare us. He said if it was a drill, he would know about it, because he was second in command after the principal, Mr. Excell. I probably asked him several more questions, trying to figure out how this was happening. I think my little kid mind was trying to eliminate all the reasons to believe it was real. Maybe realizing that it was real, I looked out the window again, wondering if I'd see FBI and sniper men hiding behind anything out there and peering through scopes into the room. I didn't see anything like that either, but it occurred to me to get away from the window so I would not be between their shot and the man with the bomb. I was beginning to absorb the reality, but only in fictional doses.

I don't remember much of what happened between those thoughts and the moment when the fourth grade class arrived, but I do remember the gloom we all felt. We all knew they were the last class to be gathered. We'd heard they were outside somewhere and I thought maybe they wouldn't be found and captured. But here they came.

I think it was after all were gathered in that David spoke up and had his "manifesto" paper sent around. It was typed on a sheet of paper with hardly any margins and I took no time to read it once I realized it seemed just plain crazy. This was the first time I had heard him say anything at all. Apparently he had done some yelling at the younger ones and their teachers before our class had arrived. He spoke in a very underwhelming voice, but gave the feeling that he did not care whether we understood his words, almost as though he expected us to not understand. "I am the most wanted man in the culture." (Yes, I do think he said "culture.") I wondered what he meant. I heard him say something about sending the letter off to President Reagan and other government officials. . . . He said other things, but I wasn't following it.

Somewhere at about this time, David had to shed his gold wind-breaker or sweater. I remember some very tense moments as we watched Doris help him take the jackets off. He carefully unwound the white ragged shoelace from around his wrist, lifted his hand slowly from the handle of the cart, and pulled his arm through the shoelace trigger, and then out of his jacket sleeve. He took a moment away from the trigger to adjust a pistol from the front of his pants and put it back. I recall he checked one or two more guns on his body. He placed the shoelace back around his right wrist and settled back into position with his cart. He remained in the middle of the room the entire time I saw him. Doris was only near David when she helped him remove his jacket, or when he called her over. She generally stayed near the main door, once she was done recruiting classes.

The smell of gasoline was getting thick, and the temperature of that room, with 154 hostages, was on the rise. Kids were throwing up in the sink or garbage cans, and asking for drinks of water. Doris made an announcement: "Kids! Many of you want to get drinks of water, but we can't have you doing that. If you're thirsty, get a paper towel wet and put it on your forehead."

My buddies and I giggled to each other from our end of the room. "How is a rag on your forehead going to help if you're thirsty?" Then Doris made another announcement: "Kids, think of this as an adventure . . . this will be something you will tell your children and grandchildren about."

One of the teachers spoke up and decided it would be a good idea to sing "Happy Birthday" to Jeremiah Moore. That song sounded dreadful. Many say they noticed David and Doris singing along, which was even more strange. Maybe *another* song was in order. The first graders were just finishing up a week themed with bears, so they sang a song I'd never heard before: "If you go out in the woods today, you're sure to get a surprise. . . ." I wondered what kind of song that was! This song thing wasn't working!

The mood was still very somber and sobs were heard around the room. Tissue boxes were passed around. I saw one of my classmates, one that is usually very mouthy, have a very uncharacteristic meltdown. He was sobbing while saying out loud, "I'm never going to see my parents again . . . they're never going to see me. . . ." At about this time I heard Brian Nate say to someone, "Heavenly Father won't let us die; we've done nothing wrong."

Although I personally had not even begun to draw conclusions about our situation, I had felt bad for the kids who were crying and I wanted to help. Brian's words made perfect sense to me—*"We haven't done anything wrong . . . Heavenly Father won't let us die!"* I immediately began spreading that phrase around the room. Brian said it in one direction, and I in the other. We said, "Pass it on!" to the kids in each direction.

Somebody suggested we should pray. I did an individual prayer silently. Then, someone suggested we say a group prayer. It seemed like a great idea and I remember moving around on my knees to gather people into a circle for a prayer. We didn't make any effort to conceal ourselves from David or anyone else; we didn't really even think about it. There were maybe about eight to twelve of us, seems like mostly fifth and sixth graders in a circle. It was about as large an opening as we could make in the crowded room. As I looked around at the circle, I saw a lot of eyes looking at me. I could only guess that they were waiting for me to either say it, or call on someone to say the prayer! I felt the obvious choice was Allyson Cornia because she had always been the smartest kid in class! Made sense to me at the time. She prayed loud enough for the small group to hear. We knelt and bowed our heads and folded our arms. She said a simple prayer—you can imagine the words. The feeling afterward was a feeling of total confidence that we had just placed our lives in the hands of our loving Heavenly Father. There was nothing left to worry about. It was like our part was completely done and it was just a matter of time. I don't even think we wondered just how long or short or how it would be done, just that it would. At least that's how I felt.

Looking back, the fact that the mood was much lighter tells me I was not the only one that felt it. This is probably the point at which they asked to remove many of the desks into the hallway to make room. Teachers had also asked if they could bring book carts in from the library and later, even a TV on a cart for the kids to watch in the corner.

Meanwhile, several of us were positioned behind a row of first grade desks near the northeast corner. We were looking at the bomb cart and how it was put together. We saw the wooden clothespins wire-lashed to the cart handle. We knew the shoelace around his wrist was important, but I'm not sure we knew it was the main trigger. We peered into holes in the paper bags and saw Duracell batteries. We conjectured together that maybe when the batteries died out, then the bomb would go off. We saw a coil of chains on a roll underneath everything, at the bottom of the cart. The milk jug with gasoline sat in the top right corner above other boxes and cans. The chains, we thought, might be for tying kids up . . . ? Turns out the chain coil was there to throw shrapnel. That detail gets me every time I think about it. . . . How can a person get to that kind of thinking?! That shrapnel, that bomb, was designed by that man to kill me and everyone else in the room!

I wanted a closer look and we kind of dared each other to go get a book from the book cart. I took the challenge and walked confidently to the book cart. I grabbed a book. I walked back, eyeing the cart to get a look and then my eyes met his. It seems he knew what I was up to. His eyes were as cold and soulless as I've ever seen. There was no light in them. He had no scowl or angry looks, just a cold stare in my direction. I moved past and felt bothered by his stare as I sat back down behind the desks with the others.

First grade teacher Carol Petersen, maybe noticing that we needed to keep out of trouble, said (in a mock enthusiasm as if we were first graders) "Hey, kids! Who wants to read about dinosaurs?" We laughed heartily, and it broke the momentary tension after my encounter.

Timelines are hazy, but at some point after the TV was brought in, Mr. Mitchell got everyone's attention and raised a roll of masking tape in the air. He said, "We are going to make a magic square here on the floor. We're going to play a game to see who can stay outside of the square. If you go across the line, you're out." He and another teacher placed a 9 × 9 foot square around David and his bomb. He was sitting on the corner of a first grader's desk in the middle of the square, under the one fluorescent white light, and faced north toward the chalkboard.

When that tape was being laid down on the carpet, I noticed some Lego blocks at the southwest corner of the square. I asked Brenda Hartley if she wanted to go over and play with the blocks. I had my back to the TV as I built a little tank with the Legos. She watched the TV and me, while fiddling with some of the blocks.

Once I had my tank built, I said to Brenda in a gruff military voice, "Okay men! We're going to go across the 'Death Line—*Vroommm*!!" Brenda laughed. I looked up at David to see if he had heard me. He *had* heard me and glared at me from over his right shoulder. As I looked up from my position on the floor, and looking past David, I noticed that the light around him and in the room was a yellow/hazy light. I wondered at it, because I knew it should be more of a white fluorescent light. This light was almost more like what you'd see in a smoke-filled room.

In the process of looking up I also noticed a crowd of fellow sixth graders gathered by the main door. Thinking nothing more about the color of the light, I nudged Brenda and said we should go see what our friends were talking about. This was my first time to this side of the room since I had arrived, and I saw just how easy it would have been to step right out the door into the hallway. I stayed inside, knowing I simply needed to. I listened in on the conversation my friends were having with Doris as she sat on the desk "guarding" the door. She seemed delighted to have our attention. Someone asked how long they were planning to keep us. She said, "Maybe ten days, maybe a month . . . depends on how long—" Drew Cornia interrupted saying, "Shoot! I just got these braces in and I don't have my special toothbrush!" We all laughed.

Suddenly, the group broke apart when David called Doris away from her post. Apparently he had called her so he could hand the bomb over to her. He needed a break in the tiny bathroom between the two first grade rooms. He needed to either use the bathroom, or was having a diabetic episode, or was disturbed with the way the kids no longer seemed nervous. Could it have been the influence of what I learned later was angels encircling the bomb? I don't know what led David to leave at that moment, but something was in the works.

I moved myself from within a few feet of the bomb to only about eight feet from the main exit. According to the accounts of Rachel and Katie Walker, they had been told by an angel that the bomb would go off "and to listen to their brother's instructions." Travis Walker, in the meantime, had heard and followed a prompting to get his sisters near the window because the bomb would be going off "soon." Their account is in direct timeline with the strange light I had noticed about ten minutes earlier. Maybe it's just coincidence, but I have to wonder if that is one more way God works in our lives. He orchestrates masterfully, even if we don't hear the orchestra or see the performers.

When the bomb went off, I remember immediately hearing my inner voice say, "The bomb!" I do not remember the sound of an explosion. My mind was so far removed from the dangers of the day, it's as if my instincts had to remind me that I needed to run for my life. Of course all this was in milliseconds of time. But time did [seem to] slow down for those moments and I recall vividly what I saw and what happened next: I was being lifted and spun around in the air, in the direction of the open door. So now I was positioned 180 degrees from how I had been, and floating (what seemed very slowly) through the air. As I spun around I saw pitch-black smoke in the far side of the room right where that TV had been set up, and where maybe most of the kids were. In front of that blackness was an orange dome-shaped fireball—not a mushroom blast shape, or fireball with fingers of flames, but a smooth edged, orange dome shape. I'm not saying that's all it was, that's just what it looked like when I saw it. It's possible that the big flash happened before I ever got clear of the tables to be able to see anything clearly in that direction.

This all was happening very, very fast, but it seemed slow to me. As I was flying through the air toward the door, I saw slow-moving pieces of paper with the leading edge in flames. I had to pull my head back to dodge them. What I wonder about today is why those pieces of paper were being blasted outward, away from the bomb, yet I was being blasted in the opposite direction toward the open hallway—The physics of that doesn't seem natural. I had always said that I was literally "blown out the door," but with other's accounts of divine intervention, I wonder exactly what was going on with me.

About this point, still airborne, I remember thinking, "The fire alarm has not gone off yet! Those little kids gathered in front of the TV in the far end of the room (where it was so black) aren't going to know to run!" My eyes turned upwards at the digital clock and intercom speaker that was above the door. "The fire alarm should be going off!" I thought frantically. Just as I was beginning to panic, the alarm went off, and I was relieved. Somehow I thought that the simple sound of the alarm was going to be the difference in those kids getting out safely! Who knows?!

Still flying through the air, looking back downward, I noticed a puff of black smoke billowing right in my direction, just a few feet off the ground. I thought to myself, "Don't breath the smoke in! Stay low! Get below it." I tried to get below it, but couldn't.

The light from the hallway was illuminating everything through the doorway. I had experienced very little darkness, but I knew how dark it was on that other side of the room.

It's possible that at this point my feet hit the ground, but it must have been a bounce more than a step because I was immediately in the hallway and in a full run. There had been no one else around at all, but once I was running north toward the main school exit, I remember seeing a first grade kid suddenly by my side and a little behind me. I don't remember his name, but I know for sure it was the kid that the fifth and sixth grade classes fought over in recess football games because he was so fast. He was short, super tough, and nearly impossible to tackle. I remember thinking, "Wow, if I stay ahead of him, I'm doing good!" I knew he was safe and running hard. It's good I was in front because when I came to the front doors of the building, I just stiff-armed them open at full speed with my sixth grader size. I knew he was close enough behind me that he'd catch the open door. As far as I know, he and I were the only ones that came out that exit.

As I ran, I saw kids piling up outside below the window of the room. I don't recall seeing smoke billow out the window. The kids were being pushed out the windows but were just piling up on top of each other! I definitely remember thinking, *Run!* According to Brad Nate, he was one of those in the pile, and he remembers hearing someone from behind him yell "*Run!*"

Still running south across the parking lot, I saw kids just pouring out the south doors of the school. I remember thinking "That's a *lot* of kids coming out those doors!" I believe the doors were propped open, so kids were able to just stream out. I saw them running straight for the fence that separated the schoolyard from the neighbors' yards toward Main Street. They seemed to be hurdling that tall fence in one stride each. I do remember seeing somebody wearing a bright yellow shirt or something. I wonder now if it may have been a fire fighter boosting them to somebody's dad on the other side of the barrier. My running legs were on autopilot still, and I may as well have been flying through the air. I was definitely not conscious of my own efforts in running.

Moving across the asphalt of the parking lot, I remember the same voice inside my head (my own voice, not someone else's) that had said the words, "The bomb!" was now saying, "I'm alive!!" The moment I made that realization, my legs were suddenly back in my awareness. In other words, I felt like I had to consciously put effort into making my legs run and not trip myself. I think whatever/whoever had been helping me through the ordeal was releasing me back into my own power. It was as if it was saying, "You're okay now." I know that was the feeling I got; I'm not so sure there were any words like that actually spoken to me.

At about this point, I was approaching the corner of the parking lot, where lots of ambulances and people were waiting. I was surprised to see them; I had no idea anyone even knew what had been happening. I was comforted to know that the outside world had been aware. A wave of EMT workers and others were approaching me, running toward the school. One EMT lady, with the most concerned look she could possibly wear on her face, looked at me as I ran past, and it was understood by both of us that I was clearly OK. I knew I was. And I'm sure I didn't look burned or black or anything. She had her arms open and was in a bent position as she cautiously approached the school grounds ready to scoop up any child that may need her first. Thinking about it now, I wonder what on earth they must have expected to see when they heard that bomb go off!

This is where my memory has a time gap. I know I must have been dazed and walking around, but I don't know for how long. However long (or short) it was, I remember suddenly hearing the fourth grade teacher, Mrs. Sparks, yell out in her powerful voice, "Fourth graders over here!" She was standing on Steve Taylor's front lawn on Main Street. Her voice and the fire drill routine brought me back to reality. Her call for fourth graders was the only orderly thing happening, and it instantly snapped me into focus. It was fire drill mode. I asked her what I could do to help.

She told me to go back toward the school and tell all the kids, not just the fourth graders, all the kids to gather on that lawn on Main Street and *not* at the school grounds as we had always practiced. I immediately nodded and walked back across the street.

Kids and people were everywhere now. This is partly why I feel like I must have had a moment of blackout because I just don't know how so many had gotten there that quickly; maybe it actually *was* that quickly! I got to the other side of the street corner and saw two kids who normally had black hair with orange frizzy/curled hair. I had never seen singed hair before.

I stepped onto the curb and saw John Miller, the band teacher, supported by two EMTs. His eyes were as wide as saucers. Something was obviously wrong, but he was clearly alert and alive. He was on the little strip of grass between the sidewalk and the short chain-link fence of whoever's house that was across from Steve Taylor's. The wide-eyed look of shock on Mr. Miller's face alarmed me, but I saw that he was being taken care of by the EMTs.

I continued on toward the school telling kids to go gather on that lawn. I looked back toward the Taylors' house. On the lawn I saw a girl being squirted off by the garden hose. Some were pouring pitchers of water on other kids. I was shocked, at first to see a girl with her pants at her ankles in such a public situation, but I also knew immediately why they needed to do that. I turned toward the school again and a kid who had played Ben in the Tom Sawyer play that we were in together just months before, called me by name and asked very calmly if his shirt was on fire or something. I said, "No." Then I gently lifted up the back of his plaid shirt and saw that the first layer of his skin had peeled away into a white ring the size of his entire back. The new skin underneath was very pink and red. I told him he was burned and to go over there where they were pouring water. We both thought it was strange that his skin was burned, but not his shirt.

More kids' faces were blackened as I got closer to the school. These kids must have been inside the room for much longer than the others I had seen up to that point. Next I saw Brenda Hartley, the same girl I had played Legos with next to the "magic square" of tape. She had worn a sweatshirt that day that had a decorated clown face on the front. It was all gray and black with soot. The eyes of the clown were made of large round plastic rhinestones. They had melted, and it looked like the clown was crying. It looked awful. But it is still something to ponder today how it must have gotten so hot inside that room for her glittery-sweatshirt decorations to melt, yet survive the fiery furnace. I told her to continue to Main Street with the others.

As I continued up the sidewalk toward the school, there were fewer and fewer kids. I figured my job [assignment] from Mrs. Sparks was done. I continued all the way to the corner where I could see the school building. Small explosions and sounds were still coming from the room. Standing on the corner, looking for more kids, an angry, wild man (a father of one of the kids, I guess) yelled out, "I'm gonna go in there and get that bastard!" The cops and other adults were restraining him as he flailed. I knew exactly who he wanted to go get, and I knew it must be a parent of one of the kids. I didn't recognize who it was, but it scared me. I thought, "This guy's just as dangerous as the one who held us hostage!" (Although his demeanor was entirely opposite of David's.)

I turned back toward the chaos on Main Street. Even more of a crowd was there by that time. I began thinking I better call my mom and let her know what has happened. Living six miles north of town, I was sure she had no idea what was going on. I needed to find a phone. I went to Steve Taylor's house, feeling comfortable there because Mrs. Taylor had been one of my Cub Scout den mothers. I used the side door to the kitchen and saw a man talking on the phone. The way he was talking, I could tell he was reporting what was happening over the radio. He began describing "blackened faces and the bomb going off just minutes ago."

I said, "Mister, I need to call my mom and tell her where I am." He closed up his report quickly and let me have the phone. I was kind of surprised he let me have the phone. I dialed and got nothing. The circuits were all busy. (All the phone circuits were overloaded for the next day or so, I think.) I could see that calling wasn't going to work. I had heard that many of the sixth graders were down at the town hall to be out of the way. I knew I was okay, so I decided that would be nice to go be with my friends and classmates, and not in the chaos on Main Street.

I stepped outside, onto the Taylors' porch, which looked over the chaos unfolding on the street in front. In the midst of it all, I saw the white Channel 2 News camera right in the thickest crowd of people. I may have even noticed their satellite truck. I thought to myself, "They got here quick!" I stepped into the crowd to find someone to tell my parents that I'd be in town hall. I wasn't sure who to tell that to . . . who would my mom and dad ask to find me?

As I was now on the far side of the crowd, I suddenly saw my dad as tall as a telephone pole coming down the sidewalk. I saw my sister Cindy and my mom. I yelled out "*Mom*!" My dad's arm shot straight up making him appear even taller. I can't imagine what they must have been feeling as they joined the chaos around them. Had they even known I was alive? What they must have felt! It was a small miracle that we found each other that quickly! They ran to me and I sunk right into my mom's open arms. She was safety and softness.

Right then was the first time I had gotten emotional all day. It all sank in at that moment that my life was almost taken. I cried.

Apparently when I had yelled, "*Mom*!" the KUTV news camera heard the yell and caught our moment of embrace. This image was repeated in newspapers across the nation and one of them was the southern Arizona paper that my oldest sister, Wendi, saw two days after the event. Still unable to get through to us by phone, the image of me wrapped in my mom's embrace was the miracle Wendi needed to know that I was okay.

After so much commotion, injured students had been carted off in ambulances and school buses to nearest hospitals (forty-five minutes away or more), I sat on the lawn with my folks and Rocky Moore. We talked about the miracle that no one had perished but David and Doris. Rocky said it was his "burning bush." He described getting his belt buckle caught on the windowsill, wondering if David would kill him right there. We strolled up to the corner again to look at the school. Officials were still moving about.

We drove home (although none of us can remember the trip) and *Deseret News* reporters followed us. My dad had worked at the "News" years before, and they were welcomed. I sat on the couch and answered questions. The interviews were interrupted when, somehow, a *New York Times* reporter got through the phone lines to our home, called, and asked my mom and dad permission to interview me. I agreed. All she asked was what my favorite subject was in school! I couldn't believe it! I have no idea what article was written, but I'm sure stuff was made up because she got no information from that interview!

Dukes of Hazzard was on TV that night. Other shows with explosions and guns were on, and I'd had enough of that already.

Saturday brought us into town on that same corner again, looking at the school building. Kids swapped stories. The rest of our friends were out of town in hospitals. My dad was the baseball coach, and we had a game scheduled for that evening. He asked me if we should cancel it. I emphatically said *"No!"* Life should go on as normal; if there was ever a time we should have the game, it was then. That's how I felt about it. But there was a problem: my baseball mitt was inside the school building! We got special permission to go in on the far north end of the building, where the sixth grade classroom was. Black smoke streaks stained the ceiling where the vents were.

The high school gym was opened up to a town meeting of sorts, to hear what psychologists had to say. Smaller breakout sessions followed in other rooms at the high school.

We held our little baseball game that evening. I played center field. The "Chopper Five" (Channel 5 KSL news helicopter) landed near the adjacent football field. I thought that was so-o-o cool! I wonder what the reporters and out-of-towners thought of that baseball game happening like that.

Sunday was interesting. There was a Channel 5 news camera in the sacrament meeting where the kids sang "I am a Child of God." We didn't hold any of the other meetings that day for church, but we met again as a town at the "New Gym" that afternoon. The crime scene had been shut down at the elementary school, which meant that we could go visit the bombed-out room if we wanted. Psychologists were recommending it as a way to see that we survived it, to show our family where we were in the room at the time.

Entering the classroom, it smelled a certain way that stuck with me for years afterward. I saw bullet holes in the bulletin board nearby where I had sat playing with magnets when the bomb went off. I saw the strange smoke markings on the east wall but couldn't make out the shape of anything mystical or miraculous. It was a strange marking on that wall, I could agree with that. We peeked into the small bathroom where we were told David had shot himself. Blood stained the floor.

We did not return to school for several days afterward. I think it was just short of a week later that they had us back in the school for just a few hours at a time. During this time, my brother took a few days to come and visit me. He was in Colorado when he saw the news on TV and just wanted to be with me. I'm glad he did. We spent a day climbing several steep hills around town in his new 4X4 truck. It was good therapy.

We moved away from Cokeville, Wyoming, to Provo, Utah, that summer, as we had been planning to do. It was a very different summer and environment from what I'd been used to on the ranch in Wyoming. For summer housing, we lived in a townhouse surrounded by college students, and next door to a pool! I spent hour after hour in that pool. At night, when the college kids were obnoxious and rowdy and playful into the later hours, my parents expressed concern. I told them I actually enjoyed the noise because it meant people were happy, and that meant things were safe out there. It soothed me to sleep. From then on, they would smile when they heard rowdy and happy college kids at night. It meant their baby boy was okay.

I was feeling independent and confident, so I asked if I could go watch the afternoon movie at a nearby theater. I had no idea what was showing, but we knew the theater had a reputation for showing family-friendly movies. Turns out the movie was JAWS 2! I sat alone in my row, near the aisle, and the exit. A man just down the way, on the other side of the aisle began to make me feel uneasy for some reason. I was in a dark room, JAWS music was playing . . . ! I really don't recall whether I left the movie theater early or not, but I don't remember the movie! I talked it over with my mom when I got home. She wisely talked me through the silly fears that had built up inside me about "a man across the aisle from me." I guess I began to see there could be a lot of scenarios that could make me fearful for the rest of my life because of what I'd been through, but that most of them would be silly and unnecessary fears.

There were times when television showed other hostage situations. They were difficult for me, and sometimes for my family too.

I was often asked to speak about the events of May 16, 1986. I was always willing to talk about it, but each time, my body would tremble and shake as I relived the events. I had nothing but good to report about the day, but there was no doubt that trauma remained inside the cells of my body or however that works.

Today, I have felt very comfortable with the story and in telling it. I have always just told it as it happened and added in all the facts I learned about afterward. I knew it was a miracle that all of us in the building were saved. Some of my friends talked about angels and miracles. And so it was.

I feel that it helps that I was one of the older kids in the ordeal and that, as a family, we had done plenty of talking about it in the subsequent years as we compiled information: a process I credit for helping me to heal from the trauma of the day.

***

As an adult, I have tried to assemble some lessons learned from this hostage-taking event. Some are lessons about this world and the way God works within it, and some are lessons I learned about myself, both good and bad. These are in no particular order:

1. Bad things can happen anywhere, anytime.
2. Not all men in scraggly beards are bad, but the eyes can tell you.
3. God allows even the most evil men the freedom to carry out evil plans. He does not condemn a man for events that lay in the future even if God may know that future.
4. God DOES intervene when we use our freedom to ask for His help. That help is highly customized.
5. As a kid, and even more as an adult, it took me a long time to realize I need to pray. I tend to be quick to pray, once nudged, but my own first instinct seems to be to investigate further, rather than praying first.
6. Miracles happen.
7. Angels are real, and evidently our relatives are among them.
8. I have a native optimism. I played; I made the most of it. I was not terribly worried, almost at any point inside that room. But I also could have been more aware of the spiritual things happening around me. I was oblivious to them, but at least I was oblivious because I had so much confidence that we'd be okay. I don't know if that's good or bad, I just recognize that it is how I seem to operate, and maybe I miss out on some very interesting spiritual experiences because I'm not paying the right kind of attention.
9. Being super intellectual is not an advantage, but a child praying with child-like faith is a super power.
10. God lives. I've noted the irony of David's philosophy that "God equals nothing," when this very story proves: "Nothing equals God."

11. The world wants to hear this story. Many, many people want the reassurance and hope that this story provides. Just because it happened to me does not mean I should keep it to myself. I've seen wonderful, helpful things happen with the telling of this miracle.

12. Anything we do in this life to set ourselves in place of God, we are in error. Asking for His help, though, and submitting to Him, can deliver miraculous results.

13. Many of my fellow survivors don't feel the same yet about sharing. Many still carry deep scars both physically and emotionally. I have learned to understand that others may have very different perspectives on things. It's good to understand that.

14. I truly am not sure if I have forgiven David Young yet, but I have faith that I can.

Appendix III

Joshua Wiscombe's Account

Cokeville Miracle

Room #4

May 16, 1986, became known in our family as "The Bomb," a day we would never forget. When you're taken hostage and your life is suddenly threatened, where do you turn for peace? We, the children, turned to God and He sent His angels to save us.

Many of us have been scarred for life by this event and many of us are still recovering. Many still weep inside, have nightmares, and shake. Some still have scars on the inside as well as burns on the outside. Many of us are grateful for the prayers said in our behalf and for the prayers of our parents who were helpless waiting at home, at work, at the high school, or in the streets outside of the school, each fearful for the lives of their children and anticipating the worst yet praying for a miracle. Many prayers came from around the world. In response to those prayers, I believe God sent his angels to protect us.

As I have had chance to talk with fellow survivors, I hear more and more of continuing miracles that happened after May 16, 1986, in their lives. From miraculous healing of burns, to voices or feelings of the Spirit at the time of the hostage crisis that warned us to move, to do something, to go or to stay. Parents felt moved to say a prayer or perform other acts of faith to protect their children. Because we were so close to the bomb, I am convinced that 154 miracles took place that day. There were unseen and seen angels there that day—some in the form of parents, firefighters, teachers, police officers, nurses, EMT personnel, and doctors; others as angels of light some of us recognized as our ancestors.

I remember walking into Room 4, seeing guns lined up against the left wall by a table. We thought we had been brought there for an assembly. Even at a young age, I realized this was odd since we had never had guns in the school before. I walked passed David, who had a bomb in a little cart in the front of the room. I was brought over to the window with my class. Mrs. Kasper was my teacher for afternoon kindergarten. I remember there were a lot of us cramped in tight against the wall of windows closer to the front of the classroom where I was. We were told to sit quietly. I could see my brother, Byron, in another class just a few people away to my left, but I couldn't talk to him. I remember being on my knees and after a bit a teacher said we would be here a while so we should try and be comfortable and sit cross-legged. I remember seeing kids crying. I remember a girl crying almost uncontrollably and the smell of gas. I remember thinking something was wrong with all of this.

Later, David had a box outline taped on the floor around him to keep us from getting to close to the bomb. "A magic square." We were told to stay out of the inside of that square. After some time had passed, I saw my sister for the first time. She was coming toward me, and she told Byron and I to come with her. I felt so relieved to see her; she was my angel. She put her arm around me, guarding me from David, like a mom, and told me, "Don't look at the scary man." I looked toward the floor. She walked me to the other side of the room near the orange cabinets.

We sat next to the Jamisons and the McNamaras. It seems like we had said a prayer as siblings and friends. I don't remember who said it. I started to understand better that this man was bad and we were hostages, which meant that we couldn't leave. Although I started to understand from my sister that we were in a bad place, I actually felt at peace. We were together as a family and close friends. We were very close to the bomb even though we were outside of the "magic square." It seemed we were on the line, next to the orange cabinets. The teachers started bringing games for us kids. We got a "Lite Brite" game. Julia Jamison and I started making a smiley face out of the glow pegs. We had just finished the smile face, and I felt very happy and actually remember smiling. I looked up and "*Boooom*"—the bomb had gone off.

I was close to the door. I jumped up and then ran to the left toward the door. I tripped over a chair. I tried to get up but began to be trampled by kids. I could feel people pushing me down. I tried to get up but couldn't. I remember it was very hot and pitch black. All I could see was flames at my feet. I tried to kick at the flames but they wouldn't go out. I remember feeling helpless and thinking, "I am never going to see my mom again!" I don't remember how I got out. The next thing I remember, I was in the hall and there was light coming from the door at the end of the hallway. I remember hitting those doors and then feeling fresh air.

I ran to my bike, which was on the opposite side of schoolyard from the street. My only thought was that I wanted to get out of there fast. To my horror, men dressed in SWAT gear and firefighters began to jump over the fence and yell at me, I didn't know they were there to help protect me, so this frightened me even more. They had guns. They were yelling at me saying, "Don't get your bike," "Just run. Get out of here." I ignored them, grabbed my bike, and took off. I began to pass kids fleeing the school. I rode my bike to the street where there were ambulances, parents in the streets, and kids with black soot all over them. Some were bleeding. Some were being hosed down, with their shirts off, to cool their burned skin. I was met in the street by my mother, (she was six and a half months pregnant) and by my sister, Steph. Shortly afterward, Byron came running over. We were emotionally scarred for life, but we were safe. We had survived "The Bomb."

I later heard that our neighbor came to tell my mother about the situation. My mother, who had three children being held hostage, and Carlene, who had two children being held hostage, knelt in prayer. These two great women pleaded with God in behalf of their children and all the children and hostages in the Cokeville Elementary, right before the bomb went off. They said their prayer, felt peace, and then walked outside onto the front porch, and "Boooom" the bomb had gone off. My mother, pregnant, ran toward the school.

Earlier that day, my father was prompted and heeded that prompting as an act of faith. Because of that faith, his children were given a miracle that protected them from harm in 1986.

I'm grateful for those who took the time to investigate the facts after the hostage crisis situation. They could see that this was a miracle, and they have declared it to be true. To my knowledge, in the history of school hostage situations, this is the only one that didn't end in a fatality other than the perpetrators. My witness is that we were saved by God. We are only here because of Him and His angels.

Appendix IV

JoAnna Wiscombe's Account

May 16, 1986, started out the same as most days, with morning chores, breakfast, and prayer. It's interesting to note that the night before we were planning a trip out of town with grandparents who were visiting, and at the last minute plans changed, otherwise my children would not have been in school that day.

After lunch, the children—Stephanie, ten; Byron, eight; and Joshua, six—left for the afternoon school. Joshua left later because of chores that had to be finished.

After waking from a rest with our youngest son, I heard the doorbell ring and a knock at the door. My neighbor, Charlene, stood there asking if I knew what was happening at the school. I said "no" and invited her in to tell me. She said, "Our children are being held hostage." My heart raced and I thought of their safety. How could such a thing happen? I ran to the phone to confirm the information, and sure enough, it was true. I suggested we pray. After our prayer, we thought we should walk over to the school where many were gathered. At the door, we heard the explosion and the sound of very loud noises going off.

It was frightening. We both took off at a run. I ran to the corner with the thought that I may have seen my children for the last time. It was a feeling of fear, difficult to express. I was out of breath and six and a half months pregnant.

I could see many people gathered, including some friends, and as I approached the entrance of the school, my daughter came running up to me and said, "We are okay!" She was covered in black with spots on her

---

clothing and with singed hair. I felt relieved and full of gratitude. Byron found me next. His hair and eyelashes were also singed. His first question was, "Mom, can we move?" Finally, six-year-old Josh came riding up on his bike, and we were all together. With gratitude, we gave thanks.

In the days and weeks that followed, we talked of the events and how they felt. We all felt a bond with each other and the people and the community, even after moving away. In reflection of this day and our children's brush with death, we are thankful that we have three children and three in-laws who have given us fourteen grandchildren who would not be here if a miracle, through the power of prayer, had not taken place. Each of our six children is a miracle, but our family would have been totally different if the events of that day had been different. This miracle was truly an answer to prayer and a building block of faith.

Appendix V

Zero Equals Infinity

The following statement is a copy of David Young's philosophy distributed to Cokeville students and teachers the afternoon of May 16, 1986. Similar copies were mailed to the press and to then-President Ronald Reagan. (His paper allowed only a half-inch left margin and ran off the page on the right side. His infinity symbols were hand-drawn.)

Zero Equals Infinity

Seemingly, some thousands of years ago, several individuals combined, or perceived their combination and therein created Man.

This creation was, and is, a concept; a thought or idea, neither right or wrong (left) but a way among ways.

For the better part of the interim then, men played with Man making love, fire, food, mores, children, Gods, language, tools, wastes, etc: combinations of divers sorts, in almost as many directions (purposes). Now people come and people go, but always as people, no longer as individuals from which people had risen (or succumb). Almost as frequently as people come and go, additional, more distant concepts (from whatever reality is the individual/that precedes them); families, clans, tribes, villages, towns, cities, states, and civilizations make their brief passages and then leave the scene.

These various combinations of Man with their various concepts of themselves invented war in order that any singular combination might achieve dominance over other combinations. This came to pass as Man attempts to preempt those rights of the individual. The individual remembers reality only in learned (rather than the original and innate, therefore false) responses to right (his combinations values) and wrong (other combinations values differing from his own.)

History is the study of these combinations.

As a matter of record, therefore, some 2400+ years ago, Socrates, an individual, addressed himself to an evolving concept called knowledge. Knowledge is again a way to conceive, but conception is enlarged through rules less combination specific. Philosophy, remote as ever, is slowly displaced by science (mathematics, medicine, astronomy, etc.), a disciplines observing the singular rule that a fact becomes knowledge when it can be proved.

Proof is a concept, it suggests something that "is" on account of itself—it "is" proven. At best a probability, at worse nonsense, proof in any event is very distant from reality. Nevertheless it has been the predominant concept these 2000+ years and any combination that has competed with other combinations using it has eventually either adopted it or ceased to exist.

Be this as it may, knowledge and its attendant proofs remain but a way among ways. Socrates, reputed to be the wisest man of his time, investigated the basis of knowledge in a manner still available (Plato wrote it down and it survives), still as viable, and still as conclusive as it was 2400+ years ago. Socrates concluded, just as we must, "As for me, all I know is that I know nothing."

Nothing? This knowledge of 'nothing' then is all we have for all the lessons of history, these 2400+ years, Christ, revolutions, insurance, relativity, moon and space probes, crusades and inquisitions, Shakespeare, Newton, medical science, hydrogen, fusion, metallurgy, Hitler, electricity, government and law, etc.?

The answer to this concern regarding the nothingness of knowledge is rather yes and no. The Knowledge of Nothing is all there is (to know), but 99.9% of us don't even know that. Mostly, as in all these several thousands of years, we believe (another concept!) we know that 2 plus 2 equals 4 or that a line perpendicular from the ground is up, or that Christ is good (bad or indifferent), or that our names or ages are such and such.

All these beliefs we accustom to call knowledge (and knowledge ordained to have been proven, yet!) we wont to impress on all combinations (peoples) for their (and our) collective salvation (moral integrity).

That our belief that the moon is something we can put men on, or that a certain creed offers a unique conclusion, or that E=MC^2 is not one whit more true than a New Guinean tribes concepts and rationales that have preserved its stone age culture into our world, leave the majority of us feeling wronged. Therefore, rather than learn the reality and limitations of knowledge, we refute truth with some age old axiom (bullets conquer stone axes), note the bobbing heads of surrounding bigots (99.9% of everyone) and retunr without doubt or question to selfish, self-centered, egotistical sub systems and social specific cultures from which we otherwise might free ourselves.

Were we to continue, however, the investigation of knowledge, we'd need to interna-lize Socrates': All I know is that I know nothing. $0 = \infty$, Zero (or Nothing) Equals the Infinite. TRUTH!

How is this to be? Believing 2pplus 2 equals 4 hardly invalidates Knowing $0 = \infty$. The diabolical trick we've otherwise learned (internalized) is realativity; when in Rome do as the Romans, when doing math do as the mathematicians, when fighting a thermonuclear war, discard spears and arrows for the thermonuclear devises, etc.

While 2 plus 2 equals 4 (and there would have been no men put on the moon if it hadn't) it might just as well equal 22 or many ('primitive' tribes frequently respond thus to any mathematical concept above 3) or various other concepts that are easier to ignore than to realize, know, and internalize. But would we internalize these various concepts, we realize the relativeness of these various formulas, that knowledge is indeed relative, therefore untrue, therefore unknowledge, certainly nothing unless falsehood.

That $0 = \infty$ is TRUE, REALITY, and a symbolic manner of rephrasing Socrates' conclusion regarding the limits of knowledge is another matter. Here we confront what we thought we pursued all these years, what we should have remembered from 2400 years ago. The imortal Greek told us, showed us, and taught us the limitations of knowledge and we killed him for it, not merely one individual once, but in all this nonsense we've engaged in since. Still, 2400 years, 24,000 years, or 240,000 eons, there is truth-relativity and TRUTH. Let's cease to be beasts and begin to be Gods!

As was suggested at the beginning of this writting, Man is an invention, he is lots of individuals. Rather or not individuals ultimately exist (and what we mean by asking that question) is matter for another writing, it will presently suffice to remember that we still singularly (individually) conceive and perceive in the ever-present. Aware of the relativity of the games we play in our various existances, we will allow our individual trajectories (precepts and concepts) their original and innate freedom to achieve their own accords (determine their own natures) without the hindrances of Man, families, clans, villages, towns, cities, states, or civilizations.

Responsible, as ever (we die our own death, remember?) for our own actions (no Man, family, clan, village, town, city, state, government, or religion condoning withholding the above noted original and innate freedoms) we will collectively evolve into the next step of wherever it is we're going (Nowhere in the REALITY of 0 = ∞ but still a long was from achieving it.).

"We are all ONE and 'we' came apart to do 'this' for something 'to do' in Nothing and Infinity."

David G. Young
4/th Oct. 1978
Tucson, Arizona

Appendix VI

List of Fourteen Factors

The following is a list of fourteen factors, compiled by bomb expert Richard Haskell and his co-investigators, which mitigated the fatal effects of the deadman's bomb designed by David Young.

1. The connecting wires to the lower set of blasting caps had been cut through cleanly, preventing battery current from reaching the caps and detonating them. This reduced the amount of gunpowder sprayed into the room on detonation by 40 percent.

2. The two blasting caps that did not detonate were placed on a lower shelf than the three that did, thus preventing them from being triggered by the bomb's heat.

3. The soft ceiling tile absorbed much of the overhead heat.

4. The two small windows were open, which helped vent at least part of the bomb's initial concussive force.

5. The two hallway doors were also open, which had a further dampening effect.

6. The tables and chairs had been moved from the center of the room, which allowed the children to more quickly escape the initial impact of the fireball.

7. No one was sitting or standing directly against the walls, where the main combustive force of the blast traveled after spreading across the ceiling.

8. None of the children were standing or sitting in the 10' × 10'

taped-off "magic square," surrounding the bomb, and were thus slightly distant from the effects of the initial explosion.

9. David Young selected, for some reason, a plastic jug that leaked; he then did not notice the leak when he filled the jug with gasoline. Further, he did not see or smell the leaking gas all afternoon, even when he was sitting or standing next to the jug. Most important, the leaking gas turned some of the explosive particles into paste, preventing their becoming airborne or igniting when the bomb went off, further minimizing intended damage.

10. Doris's body apparently absorbed much of the explosion's fury since she was standing between the bomb and the hostages.

11. The children had had a school-wide drill just the week before in the school cafeteria "on how to escape a fire quickly from a single room."

12. Princess gave an early warning to authorities, including critical details about the guns and the bomb her father had brought into the school. Civil Defense workers who had the necessary contact network to begin proper response to the emergency "just happened" to be on hand to coordinate it.

13. The hostages wisely chose to wait out the dilemma rather than risk being shot trying to escape or rushing David Young. To have done the latter would have left them more exposed to the maximum explosive force of the bomb.

14. Despite the dense smoke, the teachers did just the right thing at the right time, at the windows and doors, to evacuate all the children from every part of the room before anyone had time to succumb to the pain, fire, or lack of oxygen.

***

The following list includes a number of related "coincidences," pointed out by various people, both hostages and authorities, that should have resulted in fatalities, but did not.

- After looking at the bombed-out room, Richard Haskell concluded over and over again that, even in the partial explosion that did occur, it was unexplainable that no one died in the concussion, flames, or smoke that exploded in such a small area.
- Music teacher John Miller was shot with the smaller of the two

weapons David Young was holding, not the more lethal one. The bullet penetrated near, but not into, Miller's heart; he was out of the hospital in two days.

- Billie Jo Hutchinson's injuries put her in grave danger for weeks, yet she finally recovered. Likewise, Tina Morfeld almost died from her internal injuries, but also recovered.

- Gina Taylor's badly burned right eye healed better than anyone could predict, overturning medical opinions that she would probably have lifelong impairment from the injury.

- David Young had Eva Clark immediately in front of him and was pointing his guns at her. Yet even when she turned her back on him to shepherd her children out of the room, he did not fire on her.

- Jean Mitchell was standing next to Doris Young when the bomb went off but inexplicably escaped instantly catching on fire as Doris did.

Appendix VII

List of Hostages

Afternoon Kindergarten
Sam Bennion
Paul Clark
Heather Cory
Linzie Jo Conner
Jodie Eggleston
Jamy Ferrin
Trini Jo Himmerich
Julia Jamison
Joshua Jones
John King
Jody Pope
Bret Taylor
Gina Taylor
Joshua Wiscombe

First Grade A
Jolene Buckley
Fawna Eastman
Carl Grandy
Nathan Hartley
Hilary Larson
Joni Larson
Travis McKinnon

Jeremiah Moore
Emily Murdock
Collin Roberts
Shawn Stahl
Ryan Taylor
Katie Walker

First Grade B

Shelley Burton
Burton Clark
Jennifer Cory
Billie Jo Hutchinson
Chad Hymas
Brenna McNamara
Kevin Nate
Shiloh Pope
Heather Prows
Jennie Sorensen
Meaghan Thompson
Jeromy Lamb
Jay Metcalfe

Second Grade

Clark Bedell
Nancy Bennion
Cameron Bird
Brandon Brooks
Jennie Buckley
David Burton
Melanie Chadwick
Michelle Coates
Wade Cornia
Tareesa Covert
Jodi Dayton
Carl John Eggleston
Jason Hartley
Austin Henderson
Jamie Himmerich

Nanette Holden
Chad Madsen
Kellie Miller
Tina Morfeld
Levi Murdock
Karee Thornock
Ryan Thornock
Willie Wathen
Byron Wiscombe

Third Grade
Andy Bagaso
Jamie Buckley
Matthew Buckley
Justin Chadwick
David Clark
Joelle Dana
Ranelle Dana
Hyrum Esterholdt
Jenny Ferrin
Cindy Hartley
Billy King
Heather Larson
Joe McNamara
Chad Mitchell
Kristi Moore
Scott Mower
Aaron Roberts
Joey Sweat
Michael Thompson
Karalyn Thornock
Rachel Walker

Fourth Grade
Rusty Birch
Jerry Dayton
Dustin Eastman
Ricky Himmerich

Lana Holden
Adam Hymas
Sandy Hymas
Jeana Jamison
Joe Mackey
Jaime Metcalfe
Monica Morfeld
Jamie Taylor
Jason Thornock
Kimberly Thornock
Stephanie Wiscombe

Fifth Grade

Amy Bagaso
Janaan Bennion
Elisabeth Clark
Shaneil Cornia
BranDee Hess
Jeromy Jamison
Amber Larson
Colton McDermott
Joanna Metcalfe
Brad Shane Nate
Lori Nate
Angie Nostaja
Adam Prows
Justin Sweat
Michael Taylor
Leigh Ann Thornock
Travis Walker

Sixth Grade

Kent Cassels
Christy Clark
Tammy Coates
Allyson Cornia
Drew Cornia
Celeste Excell

Brenda Hartley
Brandi Himmerich
Paul Lazcanotegui
Kimberly Madsen
Bobbie Jo Miller
Brian Nate
Greg Nate
Cameron Roberts
Heidi Roberts
Anna Stewart
Kyle Thornock
Kamron Wixom

Teachers

Max Excell, principal
Janel Dayton
Kim Kasper
John Miller
Jack Mitchell
Jean Mitchell
Rocky Moore
Gloria Mower
Carol Petersen
Kliss Sparks

Others

Pat Bennion, substitute teacher
Verlene Bennion, teacher's aide
Gayle Chadwick, media aide
Eva Clark, parent
Kathy Clark, preschooler
Tina Cook, secretary
Cynthia Cowden, teaching job applicant
Sandy Gonzales, UPS driver
Kris Kasper, student teacher

Cokeville Elementary Students Absent May 16, 1986

Chris King, first grade
Wendy Bartschi, second grade

Vern Setser, third grade
Mandy Taylor, third grade
Julie Anderson, fourth grade
LeaKae Roberts, fourth grade

Morning Kindergarten Students (Not Involved)

Josh Anderson
Amanda Birch
Candice Bird
Zack Bird
Alex Dayton
Jessica Dayton
Chris Esterholdt
Mindi Hymas
Dain John
Sandra Metcalfe
Julie McKinnon
Ben Pieper
Brittany Swenson
James Thompson
Krista Thornock
Phillip Stoker
Jared Sweat
Regina Tso

Appendix VIII

Sources of Information

Personal Interviews and Statements:

Glen Birch family (home used by media), statement of May 18, 1986
Eva Clark (hostage/mother of hostages), interviewed May 18, 1986
Christina "Tina" Cook (hostage), interviewed May 24, June 10, 1986
Janel Dayton (hostage), interviewed May 22, 24, 1986
John Dayton (Cokeville mayor), interviewed May 24, 1986
School Principal Max Excell (hostage), interviewed May 19, 1986
Ron Hartley (investigator), interviewed May 21, 30, 1986; March 12, 1994
Jack and Jean Mitchell (hostages), interviewed May 24, 1986
Bernie Petersen (relation of Doris Young), interviewed June 10, 1986
Carol Petersen (hostage), interviewed May 24, 1986
Gwen Petersen (relative of hostage), interviewed May 22, 30, 1986
Genera Robinson (home used by media), interviewed May 19, 1986
Kliss Sparks (hostage), interviewed May 24, 1986
Steve Taylor (father of hostage), statement of May 19, 1986

Newspapers and Periodicals

Arizona Daily Star
Brigham Young University *Daily Universe*
Color Country Spectrum
Denver Post
Salt Lake City *Deseret Morning News*
Kemmerer, Wyoming *Gazette*
Las Vegas Sun

Pueblo, Colorado *Chieftain*
Provo *Daily Herald*
Mormon Trail
Newport, Virginia *Times-Herald*
Rocky Mountain News
Phoenix *Gazette*
Salt Lake Tribune
Star Valley Independent
University of Utah *Chronicle*
Utah Statesman
Virginia *Pilot*
Time Magazine

Hearings

Under the jurisdiction of Lincoln County, Wyoming, County attorney Richard Leonard conducted hearings at the county seat in Kemmerer. Hostages, witnesses, and lawmen gave testimony. Leonard announced the investigation complete on February 5, 1987.

Appendix IX

Photo Archive

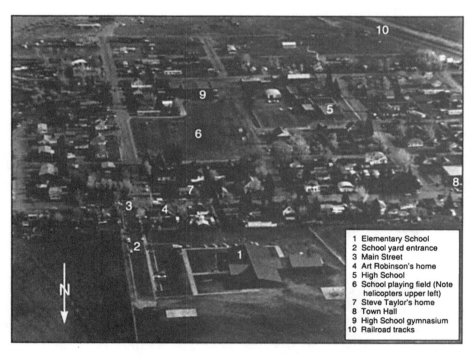

1	Elementary School
2	School yard entrance
3	Main Street
4	Art Robinson's home
5	High School
6	School playing field (Note helicopters upper left)
7	Steve Taylor's home
8	Town Hall
9	High School gymnasium
10	Railroad tracks

Aerial view of Cokeville Main Street. Library, post office, and stores are to the west (right) along the street. East across US Highway 30 is Smiths Fork Road, Pine Creek, and the town cemetery on the bluff of Big Hill. (Gerald Silver photo courtesy of *Deseret Morning News*.)

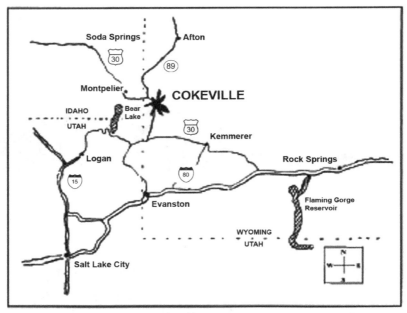

Cokeville, Wyoming

The American flag and Wyoming state flag fly briskly in the spring breeze while the body of Doris Young lies covered (white blanket) in the schoolyard. Lawmen are in the foreground.

Although his wrist was attached to the trigger of a lethal bomb, Young chose to further impress hostages with these weapons leaning against the wall of the first grade classroom. (Dan Dockstader courtesy of *Star Valley Independent*.)

David Young, a police file photo.

The arsenal collected from the school and Young's van. In addition to rifles and numerous handguns, cans of gun powder, and other bomb components, lawmen also collected three volumes of bomb construction and over a dozen diaries kept by the terrorists. (Ravell Call photos courtesy of *Deseret Morning News*.)

Town hall is the scene of a press conference conducted by Lincoln County Sheriff T. Deb Wolfley. The room is filled with television and newspaper reporters, lawmen, and investigators.

Sheriff T. Deb Wolfley explains findings of investigations to press (Dan Dockstader photo courtesy of *Star Valley Independent*.)

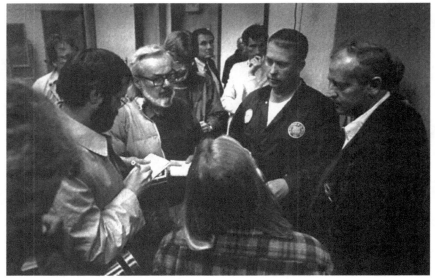

Media from across the nation question investigators on the bomb used to threaten Cokeville hostages. (Tom Smart photo courtesy of *Deseret Morning News*.)

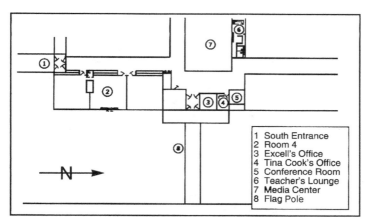

Floor plan of Cokeville Elementary School shows the south wing of classrooms, including besieged Room 4 and Mrs. Cook's receptionist desk.

Room 4. a classroom designed for 35 students that became a frightening prison for 154 hostages. Each X represents a hostage. David Young is shown in the large square. (Drawn to scale.)

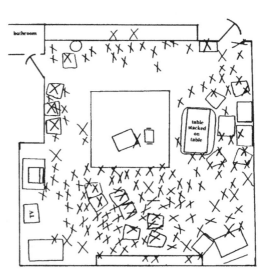

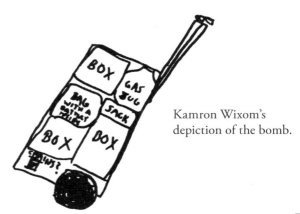

Kamron Wixom's depiction of the bomb.

1. Nathan's angel
2. door to hall
3. bomb
4. cart
5. taped square
6. hostage children
7. escape window
8. restroom door
9. Doris Young with bomb attached to wrist

Nathan Hartley's drawing.

Billie Jo Hutchinson's face says it all. In spite of the Jobst bandage that would cover her for more than a year, her smile and bright eyes promise a better tomorrow. (Jack Monson photo courtesy of *Deseret Morning News*.)

Gina Taylor manages a courageous smile from her hospital bed, although bandages swath burned face and hands. Doctors wondered if she would lose sight in her right eye—she didn't. (JM Heslop photo courtesy of *Deseret Morning News*.)

Although Jeremiah Moore's seventh birthday was not too happy, future birthdays are bound to be better. (Jack Monson photo courtesy of *Deseret Morning News*.)

Meaghen Thompson (right) is one of Jean [Mitchell's] (left) best huggers, but fear and distrust have become part of some of the children's lives since their encounter with David Young. Love strong enough to overcome those fears will be Jean's top priority now. (Ravell Call photo courtesy of *Deseret Morning News.)*

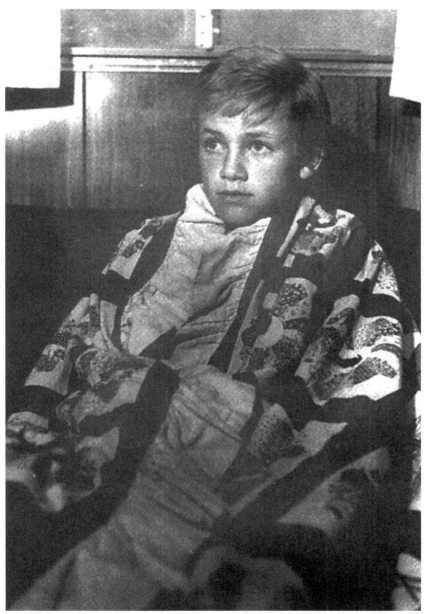

Wearing the dazed look of someone whose young life has been threatened and spared in the course of one afternoon, Kam Wixom discusses with reporters the events of an incredible day. (Gerald Silver photo courtesy of *Deseret Morning News*.) Kamron is the hostage son of the authors, Hartt and Judene Wixom. The photo was taken the day of the incident.

Rubble is all that remains of the bomb cart. The device's design was intended to destroy the entire south wing of the school. (Dan Dockstader, *Star Valley Independent*.)

Images from the Film
The Cokeville Miracle

0 26575 17611 7